SPIKING TO THE MOON

A Beginner's Guide To Understanding Whales
In The Cryptocurrency Market

Clemen Chiang, Ph.D.

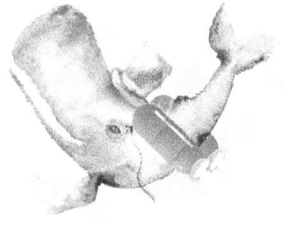

WHAT THE WORLD'S LEADING BLOCKCHAIN AND FINTECH LEADERS ARE SAYING ABOUT THIS BOOK...

This book is written by a practitioner who displayed tremendous vision, determination, and perseverance in creating Spiking Limited. You will find his personal experience and conviction as you read it.

—Tan Chow Boon,
Managing Partner, Credence Investment Pte Ltd

As a guide to crypto assets, Spiking to the Moon is simple to understand for beginners and yet contain nuggets of wisdom that experts can appreciate.

—James Tan,
Managing Partner, Quest Ventures

I have zero knowledge about the crypto space but the book really helped me understand what are the basics and how far the development in the industry has come. Wonderful book. Good job!

—Stanley Lim,
Author, Value Investing in Asia : The Definitive Guide to Investing in Asia

I was a little skeptical going into this book. I expected a lot more of the same old talk about the great days ahead of us with perfect decentralized platforms, etc., etc. What I wasn't expecting was someone that was open about talking about hybrid indexes and IEOs. Give this a read if you want to expand your knowledge.

—Houyi Chen,
Chairman, Mars Blockchain

This is a great book for crypto enthusiasts.

—William H. Nguyen, Ph.D.,
CEO, Kryptono Exchange

They say that insanity is doing the same thing over and over and expecting a different result. This applies to the crypto-banking world as much as anything. That is why it is great to read something with so many different ideas about the progression of the industry.

—Charles Thach,
Chief Crypto Officer, GIFTO

Looking towards the past to understand the future. It makes sense. There are aspects of our cryptocurrency world that we don't like to talk about. There have been a few bad apples and slip-ups. Here we are encouraged to learn from that, and I think it is a great idea.

—Rune Evensen,
CEO and Founder, COSS.IO

I was pleased to read this book and find that it didn't shy away from the security issues of crypto-banking. Rather than gloss over the negatives, this book looks at the positives and negatives to paint an interesting picture of this industry. I learned a lot. Give it a read.

—Mohamed Nasser Ismail,
Head Equity Capital Market, Singapore Exchange Limited

This book is a great resource for anyone that is a complete novice when it comes to cryptocurrencies. I had no idea where to begin or what I needed. Now I have some understanding of the first steps that I need to take towards my first investments. Thanks!

—Andrew Chen,
Managing Director, Raffles Asia Capital Pte Ltd

Life is lived forwards but understood backwards, as a wise philosopher once said. Looking back at the past to understand the future makes sense. There are aspects of crypto world that we would rather not talk about but cannot afford to ignore. Here's a book that encourages you to learn from the pitfalls so that you may navigate the murky waters with relative vigilance and confidence!

—Loo Cheng Guan,
Chairman, Vermilion Gate

"Nothing is ever set in stone in the financial world." Ain't that the truth! This book isn't going to solve all your worries and make your next trade a piece of cake. What it can do is offer some great information on the different tools and prospects within the industry. Give it a try!

—JJ Sowers,
Director, GreaterGood Society

So cryptocurrency is a fad, right? That's what we've all been told at some point in our lives. Well, now we can wave this helpful little book in front of the doubters and prove them wrong. This is a must-read account of the future of the industry. Must-read for the doubters as much as the traders.

—Charlie In,
Chairman, Raffles Capital

Huh! Mining in Paraguay?? I can now add that, and lots of other information, to the list of "things I didn't know about cryptocurrencies." This is an insightful guide that offers a nice run through of the main influences and problems facing crypto-traders today. Trust me, you will learn something too.

—Serge Kreiker,
Co-Founder, Kapitall; Co-Founder, TradeIt

There are lots of guides and experts out there that will tell us what we are meant to do with our money. They will wave some magic beans at us and expect us to take their word on faith. This offers ideas about the future of crypto with some strong reasoning to back it up. This is a realistic view of the industry and therefore pretty helpful.

—Aroop Zutshi,
Global President & Managing Partner, Frost & Sullivan

My training and career has always been in the conventional financial instruments and assets, and I found it a challenge to understand the new world of cryptocurrencies, blockchains, and the ecosystem surrounding that. Resources and references are abundant but typically tough reads. This book has helped open my eyes as a layman, and yet provided insights in a very organised run up. Thank you Clemen.

—Mah How Soon,
Managing Director, RHT Capital

The more you know about this area, the better informed you can be to make the best possible investment decisions. Reading a book like this can be a useful tool in your journey to better understand more about the whole crypto market, and the importance of making long term assessments of what does and does not hold value.

—Simon Cocking,
#1 Ranked ICO Advisor 2018, ICObench

I thought I was pretty in the know about Bitcoin, trading, and the "whales" out there. Turns out that I was wrong. This book opened my eyes to some of the different issues that are present in this crypto-world. It shone a light, and I think it will prove to be useful in the future.

—Foong Daw Ching PBM, FCA,
Former Managing Partner, Baker Tilly TFW; Former Regional Chairman, Asia Pacific Region, Baker Tilly International; Former Board Member, Baker Tilly International

The future of cryptocurrency is something that concerns anyone that is new to the industry. There are lots of scary stories out there about the dangers. That is why I enjoyed this book. It showed the problems we face and the potential solutions in a clear, thoughtful manner.

—Yee Boon Yip,
Director, MRI Moores Rowland Chartered Accountants

—Ong Jun Hao,
CEO, BlockConnectors

As something of a crypto-geek, I love to read about all the new ideas and developments in the market. I like those that are positive about the future of this industry. This book met those needs with an interesting approach and some helpful tips.

—Ho Jun Yi,
Co-Founder, icomms ICO Advisory

When I started reading this, I had my doubts. I thought that some of the concepts would go over my head. While I still have a lot to learn, this book offered a nice entry-point for me. I have more confidence now to try new approaches.

—Maksym Vysochanskiy,
Founder, BTC TV

This book paints a beautiful picture of a crypto industry where everyone gets along in harmony, there is a fairer system for the newbie and the platforms actually have an endgame. Before, I might not have believed it. Now I think that there might be something in this. Have a read and see what you think.

—Caleb Yap,
Co-Founder, Singapore Bitcoin Club

I don't normally review books like this. I skim through, take what I want, and move on with my day. This time I had to leave a review because I think that there are lots of people in my position that will be surprised by the information. You can learn a lot here.

—Henn Tan,
Chairman Emeritus, Trek 2000 International Ltd

There is a dark side to the cryptocurrency industry. We can't kid ourselves and ignore it. Instead, what we can do is look for the

"Many people believe that cryptocurrency is the future, but don't be fooled. Cryptocurrency is already here..." so true is this statement! Blockchain and cryptocurrency will impact and change the world in a big way. Start your journey with this amazing book by Clemen that not only touch on key strategic points but breaks them down and simplifies them for the reader. A great read!

—Lim Hui Jie,
Founder & CEO, ITF Corporation

An easy read and for those of you who have very little time you could always pick and choose which chapters you want to read and verify what is and what is not in crypto currencies. An intelligent how to book written in a readable style.

—Chiang Kwok Shong,
Partner, Northlands Equity Partners LLP

According to Dr. Chiang, the future of cryptocurrency and the crypto industry is a little healthier than we thought. He makes some interesting points about where we have been and where we are going. I can't say that he's going to be right about it all, but I have faith in these ideas. This is a must-read book.

—Davy Goh,
Founder, BCoin

This is a book that isn't afraid to tell it like it is. I found that refreshing. There are way too many people out there that think crypto is this perfect industry. They won't criticize it. Here we have someone that has a more realistic view.

—Andrew Fai,
Co-Chair, Asia Blockchain Alliance; Founder, OBITO.IO

Having been in the industry for a long time, i know that there are many books out there that tries to educate people about the cryptocurrency space. But none does a better job than this book.

positives and ways of improving things for all concerned. This book offers some great ideas. A must-read.

—Akhil Bajaj,
Associate Director, Frost & Sullivan

If you have ever looked at blogs about cryptocurrency and thought maybe I should give that a try, but weren't sure what to do, then this is the book to read. This guide provides helpful tips on steps to take, as well as why we should take them.

—Gauthier Bros,
Funder, Atayen

This book provides various perspective to the crypto-industry not limited to its ideas, thoughts and opinion. Its questioning style will assist readers to have a deeper thought into the topic.

—Anthony Koh,
CEO, MC Payment

This guide is a great tool for anyone that wants to learn a little more about the fundamentals of crypto-banking and its future. There are lots of factors that can affect a good trade and a good investment. Knowledge is power. That is why I recommend this book.

—Richard Giam,
Founder and CEO, Rainmakerz Pte Ltd

There are some interesting ideas in this book about the true future of the crypto-banking industry. There are ideas in here about whale tracking and user relationship that I'd never considered. I recommend this to anyone else that wants to see another side to this industry. You won't be disappointed.

—Chong Huai Seng,
Private Investor

I don't think it is too much of an exaggeration to say that this is essential reading for those that want to progress in the world of crypto. As the book says, the industry is in a constant state of transience, and we need to stay on top of trends. This is a great starting point to help us do just that.

—Seah Liang Chiang,
Co-Founder and Group Chairman, ALLID Asia Group of Companies

I highly recommend this book to anyone that has struggled with crypto-trading in the past. There is light at the end of the tunnel—according to this expert—and this book gives us the information we need to reach it. A very helpful read.

—Kenneth Tan,
Cofounder, Cezex Digital Asset Exchange

Great read, I enjoyed Dr. Clemen's objective and realistic views of the current trends in the blockchain and cryptocurrencies landscape. The book is well written and gives the reader a fresh and honest take of how this new financial tech has evolved since its creation. The analyses are clever and based on real user cases that give readers an in-depth view of the industry. I personally like Dr. Clemen's optimism and practical approach, his views are educational and refreshing. I recommend this book to all new and veteran crypto enthusiasts.

—Eric Alexandre Ceret,
Founder & CEO, Jetcoin Institute

Wow. Watch out whales! It looks like your time as negative influencers might be over. There are some interesting ideas in this book about future relationships between followers and whales. I think the author may be onto something here.

—Vitini Lin,
GM & Co-Founder, X-EVENTS GLOBAL Co. Ltd.

It was really a wonderful experience to work with Mr Clemen, so as reading this book. The content covered are hot topics and crucial for anyone interested in cryptocurrency. Definitely, a great guide book that enables a systematic and enjoyable learning experience.

—Jasmine Liu,
Business Development Director, CryptoValley

There's no better person to write a book about Whales in the Cryptocurrency Market than Clemen Chiang. He's a unique combination of a researcher, practitioner and investor, and one who analyses and reports from the trenches. His book is a must-read and a great gift for those who want to ride one of the major trends in Economy 4.0.

—Dr Patrick Liew,
Entrepreneur Of The Year for Social Contributions

I am probably meant to recommend this to new traders, given all the helpful tools in here. Instead, I want to recommend this to all those fat whales seated content in their big comfy chairs. There are some ideas in here that you could stand to read too. Give it a try.

—Leong Wei Ping,
Director, Sands Global Holdings Sdn Bhd

"This is a future where the little guy can get trading and enjoy the market too." Well, after finishing this book, I believe this a little more. This book shows that it might not be the size of the fish that counts, but the way that he navigates the water.

—Terence Kioh,
Private Investor

I have read books and guides on finances and trading in the past that went over my head a little bit. I fully expected the same from this book as I'm not familiar with all the crypto terminology or processes.

I was pleased to find that this book was written for the newcomer, not the expert.

—Daniel Chen,
CEO, CryptoValley

As a venture capitalist, we have had LPs that have came to us having a conversation around cryptocurrencies. Some were very enthusiastic, others skeptical. Then it comes down to the blockchain technology that the company uses. Many startups today use "blockchain" and force it into their business plans to raise valuations. This book gives a good understanding of what blockchain and cryptocurrencies is about, and I believe it would be a good read for other VCs so that the conversations with LPs would go smoother (because it will give a good understanding about the cryptocurrency space).

—Lance Quek,
Managing Partner, Centicorn Ventures

I will admit it—there were many terms that were completely unfamiliar to me when I first looked into crypto-banking, markets, and everything else. I tried this book in the hope that it might point me in the right direction. I was impressed with how easy it was to understand.

—Eugene Loza,
Founder, EXCAVO

One of the crypto books that most stung my interest this year — broken down into easy to understand small bits — are very different in terms of syntax and sentiment. But each implicates the reader deeply and resonates to crypto traders. Each section delivers the sense of an especially sentient trading perspective seeking to explain something that matters. Each section proposes to teach us all over again how to think, to feel, to navigate this market.

—Jack Chia,
Co-Founder, Blockchain Alliance

If you're clueless about blockchain and cryptocurrencies, and would like to find out more, this is a great place to start!

—Corinne Tan,
Principal Consultant, imPRESSions PR

"Thar she blows!" Spiking To The Moon_ is a fascinating and illuminating read, filled with information for both newbies and seasoned investors. A must read for anyone interested in the world of blockchain and cryptocurrencies.

—Ronnie Tan,
Managing Consultant, imPRESSions PR

While in no way an altruistic gesture by Spiking's founder Clemen Chiang, Spiking To The Moon does provide an up-to-the-moment understanding of the baffling and rapidly evolving world of cryptocurrency and its components. The slim guide serves to inform and educate anyone game to discover more about this relatively new phenomenon that has promised mountainous returns, and also delivered gorges of losses. Clemen does try to bring some methodology to the madness, but it's never an easy task when there are so many moving parts and new variables that rise up in the process. By presenting the evolving ecosystem, he aligns the pieces of the jigsaw, offering researched information and a history lesson for newbies to grasp the essentials of this new medium of trading.
A lot of it is foundational stuff for anyone trying to test the uncharted waters of cryptocurrency. Clemen uses his Spiking algorithm to explain his rationale for swimming with the big whales in an uncertain current.

—Kannan Chandran,
Publisher, STORM.SG

CONTENTS

Foreword -- 15

Introduction -- 17

The 3 Best Written White Papers for ICO -------------------------------- 21

The Best Bitcoin Exchanges In The US With Bank Transfer From Singapore --- 27

Bitcoin, Will It Spike? -- 35

Will It Moon? -- 47

Why Crypto-Friendly Banks Are Vital To The Future Of Cryptocurrency ---- 53

STO Tokenization Could Shape The Evolution Of Crypto-Banking ---------- 59

Does The Stablecoin Have A Secured Place In Cryptocurrency Right Now? --- 65

Will February 27th Be The Turning Point For Bitcoin ETFs? ------------- 69

Is Ethereum's Place In the Cryptocurrency Ecosystem Secure? ----------- 73

Token Swaps In The Evolution Of Cryptocurrency ------------------------ 79

Why It Is Vital For ICOs To Have An Endgame --------------------------- 83

China's Growing Role In The Cryptocurrency Market --------------------- 89

The Potential Significance Of Binance Singapore ----------------------- 93

Which Crypto Companies Are Pushing Forward Towards IPO? --------------- 99

The Growing Threat Of Unauthorized Crypto-Mining In Crypto-Exchanges --- 105

How To Participate In An ICO Public Sale? ---------------------------- 111

The Growing Popularity And Worth Of The Initial Exchange Offering ---- 115

Crypto & Stock Index For Investors ------------------------------------ 119

Using Spiking To Understand Those Whales ------------------------------ 123

How Spiking Can Bring The Best Of Crypto-Banking To New Users --------- 127

Conclusion -- 131

Acknowledgements -- 135

About The Author -- 137

References -- 141

Permissions --- 147

> Just as it got easier to use email, it will be easier to use Bitcoin as people invest in it and become familiar with it.
>
> —GAVIN ANDRESEN

> Somehow I wound up with the nickname 'Bitcoin Jesus,' so people expect me to know about everything everywhere.
>
> —ROGER VER

Foreword

I met Clemen during a meeting set up by mutual shareholders. Having conducted some, invested in a few, and assisted many Initial Coin Offerings (ICOs) prior to that, they thought it wise for me to advise his startup on the perilous journey of an ICO. On hindsight, perhaps they meant for me to dissuade him, but the unintended effect was to have connected two entrepreneurial misfits that fateful day.

We became fast friends on our shared faith, chemistry and just the sheer lack of understanding of what failure meant - the perfect ingredients for the journey that lied ahead.

To say that the journey was eventful would be a complete understatement in every way possible. The inside joke was that if there exists a true definition of an "ICO Advisor", Clemen would be the epitome of one, having gone through EVERY permutation of difficulty that an ICO may go through. Oh, and he succeeded too!

Clemen embodies a strong sense to give back and contribute to the community, particularly in the area of education. It is with his passion (or should I say obsession), that Spiking was created, having taught extensively in trading and market analysis for more than a decade. Naturally, with a transition into crypto-markets, Clemen quickly developed Spiking to deploy algorithms in tracking whale trades/movements. As with his award-winning technology startup, Clemen compiles his specific knowledge from success and delivers it in a succinct manner in this book.

For a trader/investor, I think that this book is a gem of a read, as it offers insight and perspective into the inside world of how crypto markets move, from an author who has been deeply involved in traditional markets. More so, it comes from the keen understanding of a token issuer (the genesis) and how a token navigates from conceptualisation to secondary markets. It covers current industry development well, from the ideation of Security Token Offerings (STOs) as well as the trendy topic on stablecoins.

For me, this book has proven invaluable. Apart from being a knowledge bank for educating others on crypto, it is a strong reference point to align on my investments going forward. Regardless of your level of expertise or involvement in the crypto markets, I'm sure you will find it as critically informative as I have.

—JEREMY KHOO
Managing Partner, CRC Capital

Introduction

Many people would say that everything about cryptocurrencies and crypto-trading is futuristic. There are fiat traders and technophobes outside of the digital age that still see blockchains, cryptocurrencies, and ICOs as tech that is ahead of our time. This isn't the case at all. Those that have been sleeping on this new market simply haven't noticed its growth and development in recent years.

When we talk about the future of cryptocurrency, we don't mean some distant, highly advanced system on the horizon. What we mean is the ongoing growth and development of an established industry. Bitcoin isn't the future. Instead, it is the old, dependable option with newcomers snapping at its heels. ICO public sales aren't revolutionary. Instead, they are an everyday part of the system. Looking to the future means looking at ways to improve these systems, create better platforms, and expand into new areas.

In order to consider the future of cryptocurrency, we also need to look at the past and the present.

We need to understand the issues that have occurred in the past, as well as the current successes and failures that drive the industry forward. By looking towards the past, we can see the reasons behind some the fears and negative issues that still plague the industry. We see why there are so many fears about security and regulation because we see the long lists of failed projects and rejected applications. We see the past crashes in leading currencies and the threat that this may happen again.

By looking at the present, we can see areas where we need to make a change or nurture ideas. This means issues of security, improved regulations and with the general reputation of the industry.

Blockchains, ICOs, and crypto-banking may be long established, but there is still that sense of uncertainty and general lack of trust. While some companies push forward with their vision for a brighter, cleaner cryptocurrency ecosystem, others feel that things have stagnated. Then there are the concerns about the whales and their impact on this bad reputation and stagnation.

By looking to the future, we can create a long-term plan and a better vision for the industry. This means new approaches and markets where developers can invest and grow. ICOs need long-term goals to develop their currencies and tokens. Governments need to be able to fund projects and relax laws to encourage growth and stability. There are platforms out there that are ready to take over and push the industry in a better direction. Notions of whale tracking, investment in new territories, and secure IEOs are sure to help.

This book is designed to take you on a journey through these different issues.

Here we can explore the past, present, and future of cryptocurrency and see that there is a bright future for the industry. This is an industry that is in a constant state of development and change. That doesn't mean that all the changes have to be negative. For every company that fails to create a strong strategy, there is a skilled team ready to transform the market. For every close-minded government and regulatory board, there is another ready to seize the day and embrace cryptocurrencies. There are bound to be similar spikes and crashes, and there is also a gamble in trading on the markets. Still, there is no doubt that future platforms and exchanges can be less volatile.

By the end of this book, you should have a better understanding of the industry and how you can take advantage of its growth. This future that we envision for crypto-banking isn't one that is exclusive to the giant whales and experienced traders. This is a future where the little guy can get trading and enjoy the market too. As you will see at the end, we also see a world where whale tracking and user-friendly secure systems have us all working in harmony. This may all sound like a pipe dream at the moment, but this is actually a reality right around the corner. Before we learn more about this future opportunity, let's learn a little more about where we are at.

 Every good ICO and crypto-platform needs a strong white paper.

We all want the best trades, tokens, and currencies, but there is rarely a "sure-thing." We need to be sure that any company in this industry understands everything about the purpose of their product, the cryptocurrency they use, the tokens offered, and the exchange system in place. They also need to know where they are going, what their immediate future entails, and the projections for the platform. There is a lot to consider, and this all needs to be articulated in a clear, professional document.

Here are the 3 best written white papers for ICO to show you what we mean.

When the Bitcoin white paper emerged in 2008, it was completely revolutionary. The amount of concepts that had to come together in just the right way - computer science, cryptography, and economic incentives - was astonishing.

—FRED EHRSAM

Chapter 1

The 3 Best Written White Papers for ICO

Gaining insight into a few successful ICO projects will help to explain what all is required to work up a winning ICO document. Here are 3 best written white papers for ICO that will help.

EOS
EOS is a wonderful blockchain platform that has already raised $4.1 billion. The white paper addresses the failures of current blockchain platforms and explains how latency issues will be mitigated by dividing each block into different threads and transactions. It describes that the project supports smart contracts, integrates a governance model, increases transactional throughput, and goes for a proof-of-stake consensus protocol.

FileCoin

The Initial Coin Offering of Filecoin collected $257 million with its winning white paper that looks quite like an extensively researched article. Loaded with schemas and formulae backing the different aspects of the project, this white paper not only provides concrete evidence to support its offering but it does so in an easy-to-follow fashion.

Monetha

In less than half an hour, Monetha raised $37 million, featuring a thorough white paper that describes the great project of payment system for the blockchain. Right from the working plan, to utilization plans, from token economy to service records of the team members —the white papers have got it all. Comprehensive diagrams and product architecture descriptions work even more in favor of the project.

The Key Elements of a Winning White Paper for ICO

The white paper works quite like a detailed representation of just about every aspect of your project on paper. It should convince your audience as well as capture the interest of the investors in order to make them support your idea. Below are the key sections of a professional white paper that'll describe the objectives, the team, the features as well as the legal issues associated with your project.

Addressed Problems

The foremost part of working up a winning white paper for ICO is describing the problems that your project is going to address. Emphasize why the market needs the proposed project while identifying with the troubles that the users face on similar platforms.

The Solution

With so many projects and proposals being made, your white paper should make your project stand out by explaining why it is different from the solution being offered by your competitors. Explain how your idea can benefit the target audience, discussing the market opportunities, the business model and marketing strategies, development visions, and first users of the project.

Startup Team
Undoubtedly, a crucial part of your white paper is the description of the team members. Make sure you talk about the team members and advisors in terms of their backgrounds, qualifications, and experience in ICO or similar projects. Multi-professional teams with success stories ensure your project makes an impactful impression on the investors, especially if you include some industry experts in your team.

Token Utilization and Economic Considerations
Your white paper should explain thoroughly about the utilization of the funds raised. It works wonders if the project describes the distribution of tokens, the methods you will adopt for sales, dates of exchange listing, the date of launch of sales, redemption terms, and security guarantees. Even the unused tokens must be addressed by explaining whether they will be recycled, sold or burned.

Future Development Plans
What builds the trust of users as well as investors is a clear plan for future developments that your project is expected to showcase in the next 12 to 18
months. Some key elements of the plans may be a beta version launch and listing on an exchange.

Legal Framework Concerning the ICO
The blockchain technology and its rapid growth make it imperative to discuss the legal jurisdiction and regulatory concerns of your initial coin offering. Include information relating to legal rights, the knowledge required, token acquisition risks, a detailed disclaimer, governing law and arbitration, and warranties to make the investors and users secure.

Most investors prefer a white paper that is detailed yet simple. Showcasing pictures or diagrams that concern the subject makes it easy to understand and cuts the time spent on going through long information pieces.

Marketing and PR Strategies Essential to the Success of the ICO

It's as essential to have effective marketing strategies to make the ICO a hit as it's to have an efficient project and winning white paper. Your marketing and PR material should be convincing enough for those who have an in-depth knowledge of cryptocurrencies, as well as those who aren't very knowledgeable about blockchain technology. Social media definitely tops this list, so you must pay special attention to specialized forums, thematic subreddits, Quora discussions, LinkedIn professional groups, and Facebook groups to promote your project. Preparing email lists and updated websites and publishing news in blogs, press releases, and digital currency magazines will not only make users familiar with your project but also build the trust of investors.

 These white papers are an informative starting point.

Of course, if you want to enjoy the very best deals and in this cryptocurrency world, you need to be sure that you have access to a reliable currency exchange. Understandably, many traders stick with Bitcoin as their currency of choice. There are three Bitcoin exchanges that are highly recommended for those starting out.

Let's take a closer look at the best Bitcoin exchanges in the US with bank transfers from Singapore.

Cryptocurrencies allowed non-custodial exchange, without users having to sign up or create accounts.

—ERIK VOORHEES

Chapter 2

The Best Bitcoin Exchanges In The US With Bank Transfer From Singapore

Brief introduction to Blockchain technology
Blockchain is a distributed network of ledgers that are open and immutable, meaning that when updates or transactions are made on the system, they can be seen by everybody and cannot be tampered with.

Bitcoin uses this technology to ensure that currency exchanges are decentralized and global in nature, through blockchain you can send Bitcoin to and from any country in the world without worrying about any government restrictions or bureaucracies.

Nowadays, it's possible to transfer Bitcoins (BTC) from the US to Singapore bank accounts thanks to BTC exchange service providers. These websites allow you to send the digital currency from foreign countries and get it in any real-world denomination that you may want, such as US Dollars or the Singapore dollar.

Below are some of the best Bitcoin exchanges available between Singapore and the United States. They have been ranked based on merits such as currencies accepted, past user experiences, transaction fees, liquidity, speed, security, and customer support.

1. Coinbase

If you are based in Singapore, then Coinbase is without a doubt the most viable way to buy BTC with fiat currency. It provides you with a variety of payment methods that can be used to purchase the digital currency and other virtual assets using fiat currencies.

The first step to using Coinbase is creating an online wallet where you can safely store the virtual money. Next, you'll have to link your bank account, credit card or debit card so as to exchange digital currency directly into and out of your native currency. Once this process is complete, you can now buy digital currency to start using it locally.

Coinbase changed its sending limit from daily to weekly, and users now have a weekly limit of 10,000 US Dollars or an instant limit of 2,000 US Dollar. Moreover, buying cryptocurrency with a debit or credit card is subject to a 500 US Dollar weekly limit. However, upon purchasing 1,000 US Dollars' worth of BTC or more, then that limit can steadily be lifted.

Advantages:
a) The Coinbase virtual wallet works on Android and iPhone mobile apps, as well as your web browser
b) Secure storage. Your Bitcoin will be kept in a safe offline storage where hackers can't easily gain access

c) Insurance coverage. All digital currency stored on the server has an insurance policy from Coinbase

d) Recurring purchases. You can invest in Bitcoin slowly over time through scheduling weekly or monthly buys

e) Zero chargebacks and fraud. For online traders, Coinbase verifies most BTC payments in just a few seconds with no chargebacks, meaning the costs associated with virtual fraud are greatly minimized. You can also issue refunds to Bitcoin customers using the simple Coinbase API call

f) Instant payments. Once payment has been initiated, you'll receive money in your bank account within a period of 2-3 business days

Disadvantages:

i) Little privacy. The platform may track how you spend your Bitcoin

ii) Few payment methods

2. Belfrics

Belfrics is a beginner-friendly BTC exchange platform that's available in Singapore and other Asian countries such as Malaysia, Hong Kong, Indonesia, and UAE. To use this service, you must first register and create a Bitcoin wallet that's absolutely free. You will require a password and username to do this, and upon completion, your account will be live in just a few seconds.

The next step is to add funds to your account through cash deposits, bank transfer, and other accepted payment modes. Once this step is complete, you can now add your preferred bank account to start receiving payments, though before sending in any payments, Belfrics will first have to verify your account.

Once the appropriate bank account has been linked and the funds deposited in your wallet, you can now begin trading with Bitcoins. Belfrics will keep you updated about price fluctuations in the cryptocurrency market, while also giving you tips about the prevailing rates at intervals of trading. You will be able to receive payments directly to your verified account. One main benefit of Belfrics is that you can use your smartphone as a digital debit card at 1000s of merchant points globally.

On Belfrics, each customer can make a maximum Bitcoin purchase equivalent to 786.50 US Dollars per day and a monthly maximum rate of 23,595.00 US Dollars.

Advantages:
a) Fair market. The exchange platform's spot exchange classifies orders based on price/period priority, with no counterparty risk-factor included since all trading spots are fully funded
b) Intelligent algorithm. Through optimistic fund locking, your funds will remain free until execution with the possibility of withdrawing them at any time of your choice
c) Well-proven technology. Belfrics is equipped with DNS failover technology that offers DDoS resilience and quick failovers. Moreover, distributed server construction with clustered persistence allows for zero-outage service
d) Geo IP routing offers ultrafast access to the exchange platform for global customers
e) Exchange summation. Belfrics will aggregate the feed of different exchanges to provide you with a deeper pool of liquidity, which can be used for effective trade execution

In addition to the above benefits, the exchange platform also provides various incentives to users such as free 10,000 Satoshis upon sign-up that can be converted to cash.

Disadvantages:
i) Higher than usual trading fees
ii) Sometimes creating an account can be problematic

3. CoinMama
If you are in Singapore, then the best way to purchase Bitcoins using a credit card is with CoinMama. They accept both credit and debit

card transactions from MasterCard and Visa, plus you can also buy BTC through Western Union.

CoinMama makes it fun, simple, and secure to buy digital currency from Singapore and the US. It gives you total control of your money since there are no hidden fees, middle-men or fine print to contend with when making your transactions.

The first step to using CoinMama is choosing your preferred payment method. You can use your credit/debit card to pay online within just a few minutes, or alternatively pay with cash by picking the other available methods of payment.

For card payments, you must fill the available payment form out by following the given instructions, while for cash transactions Western Union is the accepted method.

Next, you'll have to complete the payment process and verify your wallet address by clicking on the link in the confirmation email that CoinMama will send you. Once the payment has been received and verified, your coins will immediately be availed to your wallet. Moreover, through the "My Account" dashboard you'll be able to keep track of the status of your transactions at all times.

CoinMama allows you to make BTC transactions of up to 0.421089 Bitcoins per day, which has a value of 4025.95 Euros or 5001.32 US Dollars.

Advantages:
a) No deposit is required to send coins to any wallet of your choice
b) Fast-track verification system. CoinMama has a dedicated verification team that operates round the clock to ensure secure transactions
c) A responsive customer service team that you can count on in case of any questions
d) Very high purchase limit

Disadvantages:

i) High fees of roughly 6% when buying Bitcoin through a credit card

 Bitcoin is the currency of choice here because it is a consistent industry leader and a household name.

Still, that doesn't mean that it is immune to spiking. The currency has spiked significantly since 2010, which means it has had giant peaks and crashes. Keen traders and whales are sure to have noticed that there was a massive 80% spike down from $19,000 to $3,800 between December 2017 and December 2018. This is a volatile market with dramatic changes that reflect the values of the currencies and activities of the traders. It is this risk that adds to the appeal for many traders.

So Bitcoin, will it spike?

WILL IT SPIKE

> It's completely reasonable, even if some Bitcoin currency purists wouldn't like it, to have credit and debit card payments denominated in Bitcoin rather than dollars, and net settled on Bitcoin instead of on Fedwire.
>
> —NICK SZABO

Chapter 3

Bitcoin, Will It Spike?

Since 2010, Bitcoin had spiked a total of seven times. Spiking up ranging from 5X to 500X; whereas spiking down above 90% for two out of the three bear runs. Is this trend sufficient knowledge for us to predict the next spike?

Let's take a deep dive to unravel the prophecy.

#1 Spike 🚀 500X → $0.06 Oct 2010 to $30 Jun 2011

All it takes is just 8 months to deliver an astounding 500 times return. Put it plainly, a $2,000 investment will turn you into a millionaire. But this part of the history is not going to repeat itself unless we understand how the remaining spikes evolved. Remember, this was 8 years ago…

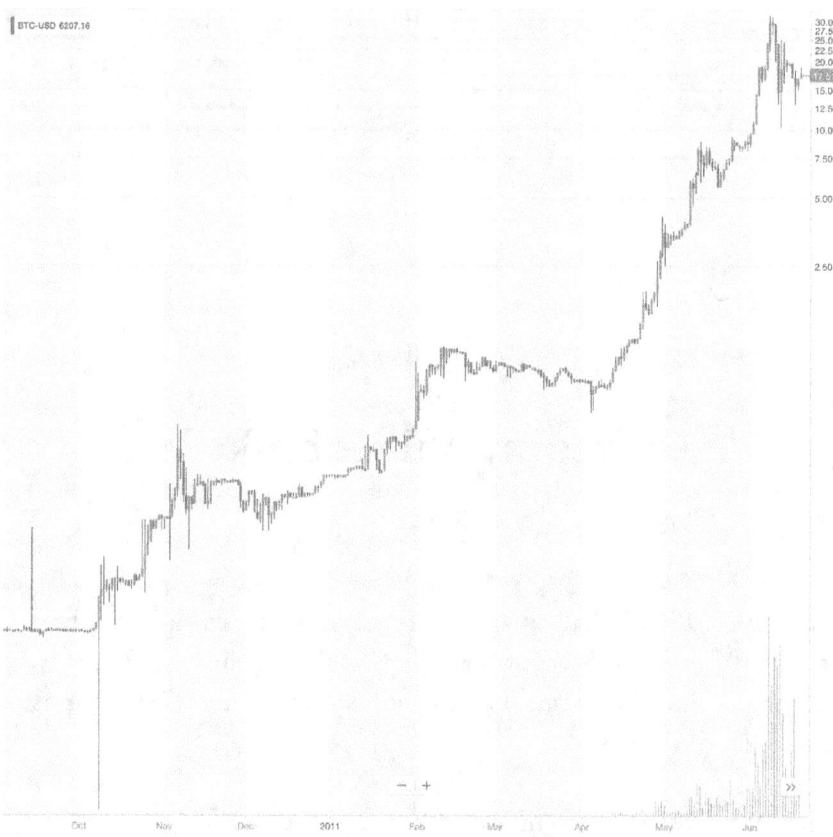

$0.06 October 2010 to $30 June 2011

#2 Spike 🔥 -90% → $30 Jun 2011 to $2 Nov 2011

Massive crash at more than 90% its high of $30. But it didn't break the support at $2. In retrospect, the initial pool of traders at 6 cents still enjoy a remarkable 30 times return. Chart-wise, you are looking at a 45-degree down trending line before the bounce off at $2.

$30 June 2011 to $2 November 2011

#3 Spike 🚀 115X → $2 Nov 2011 to $230 Apr 2013

Compared to #1 Spike, this second bull run took twice the amount of time (approximately 17 months versus 8 months) to hit the peak and delivered 115 times return. Now, the chart shows a sideways moving line with a subsequent "hockey stick" 45-degree up trending line.

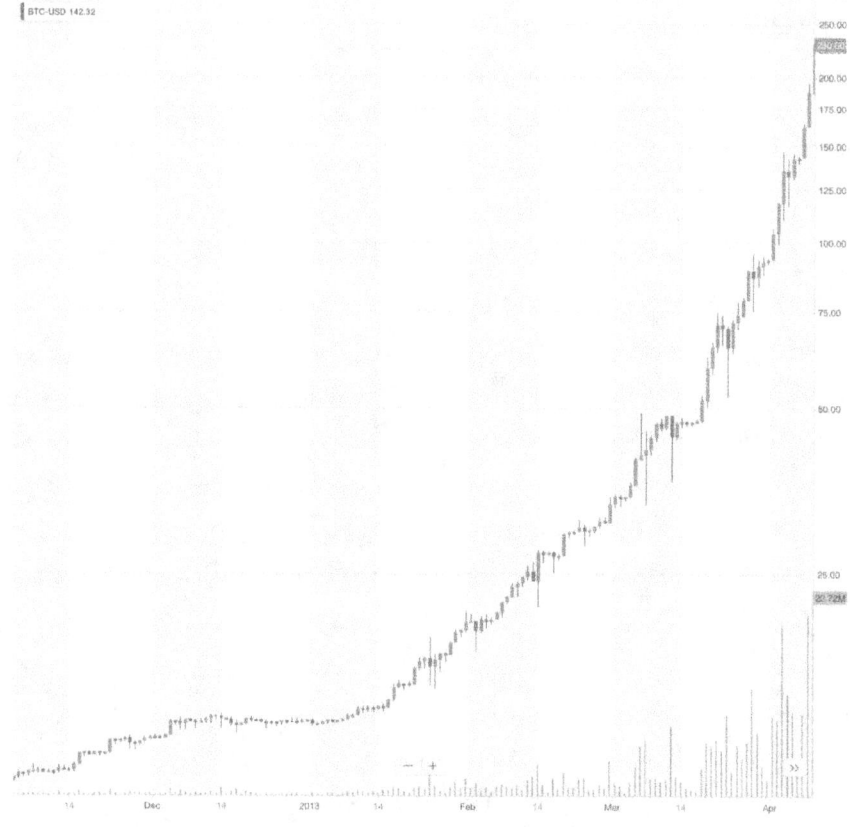

$2 November 2011 to $230 April 2013

#4 Spike 🚀 5X → $230 Apr 2013 to $1,240 Nov 2013

Compared to the previous #3 Spike, both are looking almost identical! Sideways moving lines leading to a "hockey stick" climb. But the duration is shorter at 7 months compared to the previous 17 months' wait. Here's the interesting part. What if we combined #3 Spike and #4 Spike together? It's a two-year holding period that transformed $2 into $1,240. A 620 times return, which is more than the 500X in #1 Spike.

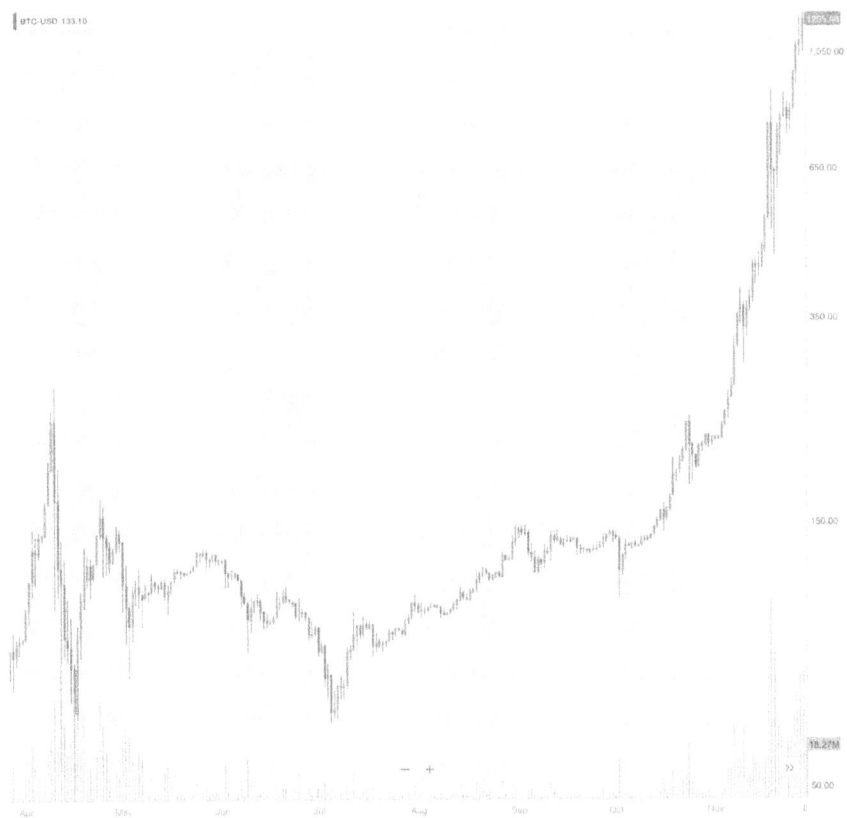

$230 April 2013 to $1,240 November 2013

#5 Spike 🔥 -90% → $1,240 Nov 2013 to $100 Feb 2014

This is déjà vu to #2 Spike! More than 90% crash with a shorter time period of 3 months compared to the previous 5 months. This serves as a reminder to all of us that crash literally means crash. It is fast and furious.

Tattoo this message on your heart!

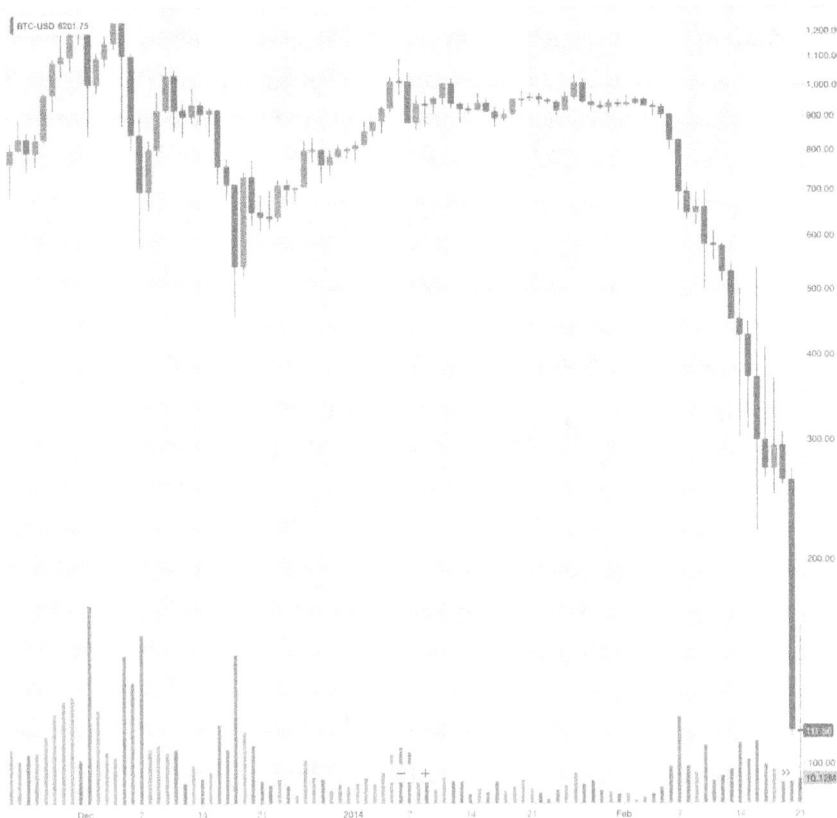

$1,240 November 2013 to $100 February 2014

#6 Spike 🚀 190X → $100 Feb 2014 to $19,000 Dec 2017

Final reminder of the *sideways moving line leading to a "hockey stick" climb.* Longest wait over 46 months that delivered 190 times return. In comparison against #3 Spike & #4 Spike versus #1 Spike, this 190X is the lowest return (620X versus 500X respectively) with the longest wait 46 months (24 months versus 8 months respectively).

P.S. 500X → 620X → 190X → ???X

P.P.S. 8 months → 24 months → 46 months → ?? months

Perhaps, this sets the stage for the next bull run? We will have to expect a much lower return with an even longer waiting period.

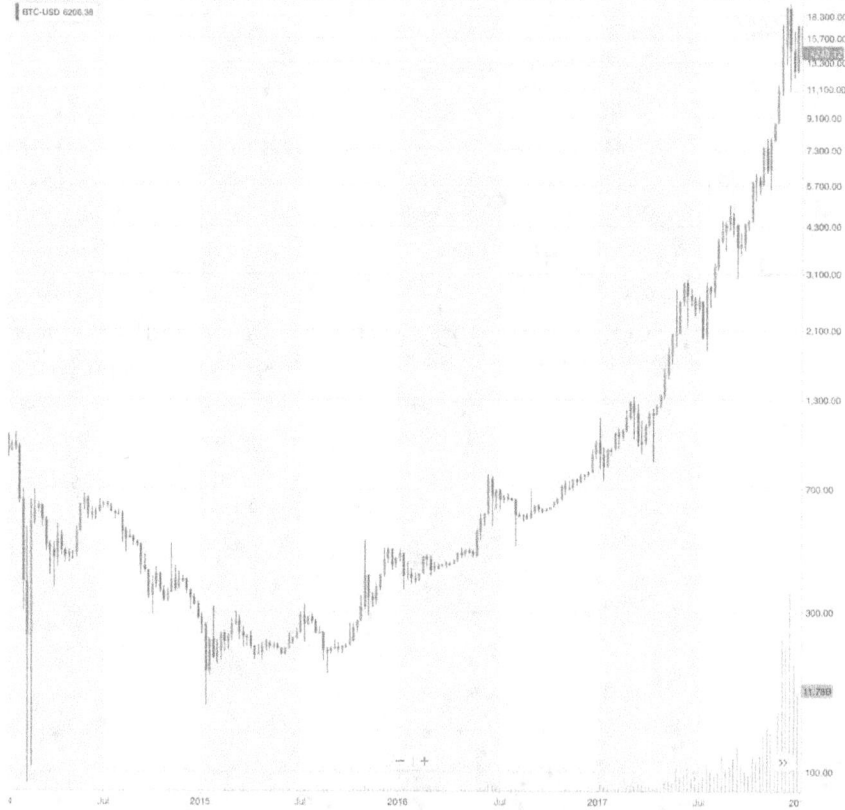

$100 February 2014 to $19,000 December 2017

#7 Spike 🔥 -80% → $19,000 December 2017 to $3,800 December 2018

If we take the two previous precedents of crashes (#2 Spike and #5 Spike), we should expect a drop of 90% from the high of $19,000 to hit rock bottom at $1,900. But hey! Previous two crashes took between 3 to 5 months to reach support levels. This time around, we are down for more than 12 months, and yet we still do not see the light at the end of the tunnel. Looking at the chart, it is not "clean" like the previous two down trending 45-degree lines.

Must we wait for the price of Bitcoin to trade at $1,900 before the dust settles?

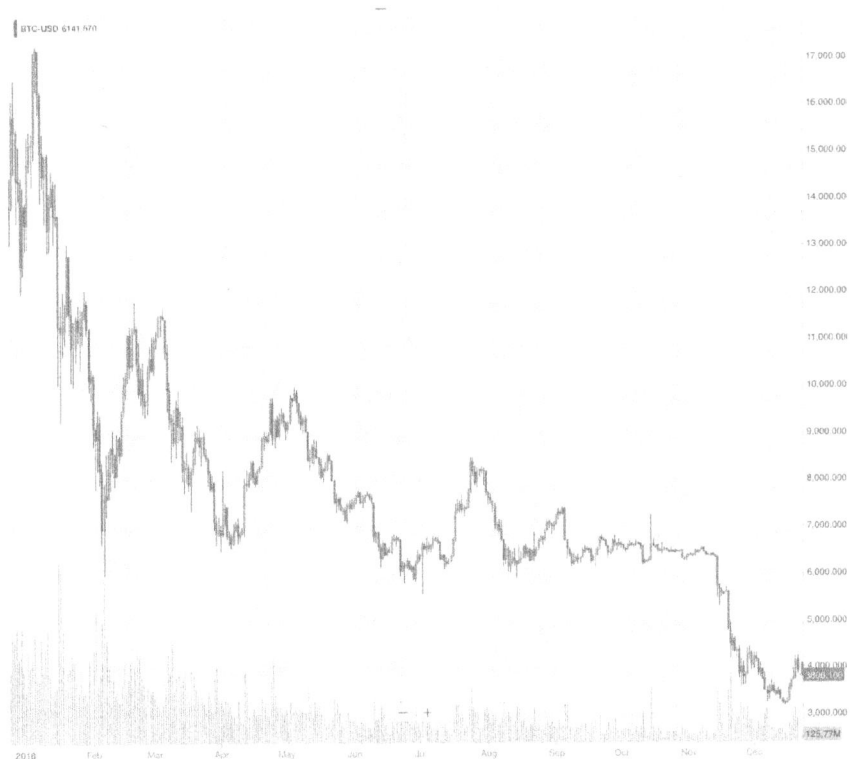

$19,000 December 2017 to $3,800 December 2018

In the final analysis, I believe that the endgame depends very much on "old money." Will the very rich consider Bitcoin or cryptocurrencies as part of their portfolios? On this note, the team at Spiking is watching the portfolios of billionaires, millionaires, and whales very closely. This, I believe, is the key to unlocking the fullest potential of Bitcoin pricing.

 It is important to remember that everything about the cryptocurrency world is transient.

There are great forces of change at work on all sorts of currencies, companies, and exchanges. Yesterday's must-have token or exchange platform could be on the scrap heap within a month. Others may be yet to find their feet. We saw this happen this year with COSS - Crypto One-Stop Solution. What was once a small, underdeveloped, and underfunded team turned things around with a new design, development team, and marketing strategy. They proved that not everyone is here for the short-term gains.

Some are out to thrive. So, will it spike, or will it moon?

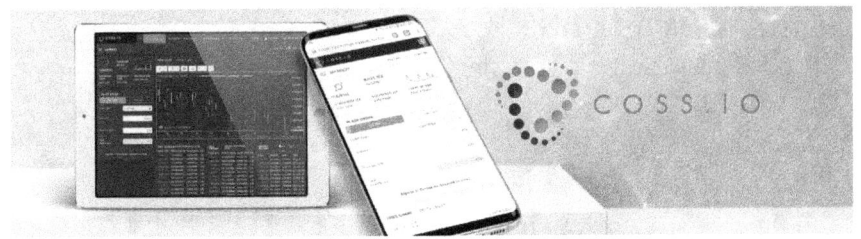

> At Coinbase, our first priority is to ensure that we operate the most secure and compliant digital currency exchange in the world.
>
> —BRIAN ARMSTRONG

Chapter 4

Will It Moon?

How to generate profit from a cryptocurrency exchange?
The only question you need to ask: WILL IT HAPPEN?

I have taken a look at the Singapore based cryptocurrency exchange. So far, my conclusion is that it might just be one of the most undervalued tokens/exchanges in the entire industry. Here's how I connect the dots together.

Some of the reasons COSS is at an all-time low:
1. Very poor Dev team
2. Very slow response time for fixing issues related to Dev
3. Little to no marketing
4. Underfunded due to a very small ICO

(raised on 3M USD)
5. A poor performing platform with multiple serious issues

What has changed:
1. COSS has now teamed up with one of the most solid Dev teams in the industry. Proven by the fact that they have already built and now operate a crypto exchange with 50M per day volume with a super smooth and fast architecture. The combined new team with all the recent new hires in-house at COSS HQ in Singapore is fully focused on building COSS 2.0 (estimated to launch early Q1 2019).
2. Complete redesign and new build from scratch with the aim of becoming one of the fastest and most stable exchanges on the market.
3. Massive marketing plan scheduled for the 2.0 launch.
4. The new venture also makes COSS financially strong enough to build through these hurdles and deliver a state-of-the-art product.

All of the above are simple facts and don't necessarily set COSS apart from many other exchanges out there. However, the token model of COSS in itself does.

With a new solid platform, I see no reason why COSS exchange shouldn't go to 50M/day trading volume. Although today's activity is very low, they still have a huge following. Many COSS token holders are monitoring the evolution of COSS, but they prefer to trade elsewhere due to the current state of the platform. These traders will be fairly easy to bring back once positive news start to hit the market.

Let's look at some historical numbers. The cheapest buy-in during COSS ICO was around 3.5 cents. Today, it is trading just above 5 cents. In itself, a decent investment for the early birds. At the December 2017 peak (entire market), COSS token reached 3.20 USD with a daily trading volume of only 12M USD. But let's totally forget about the trading price of the COSS token for a while. The ONLY interesting thing is the trading volume combined with the FSA (fee split allocation)...

COSS has just announced the implementation of a new trading fee structure.

30 Day Trading Volume (USD)	Maker Fee	Taker Fee
0 - 250K	0.14%	0.20%
500K	0.12%	0.18%
1M	0.10%	0.16%
2.5M	0.08%	0.14%
5M	0.06%	0.12%
7.5M	0.04%	0.10%
10M	0.02%	0.08%
15M	FREE	0.06%
20M	FREE	0.06%
25M	FREE	0.06%
50M	FREE	0.04%

Let's make some assumptions.

☞ COSS focuses a lot on new ICO tokens and the following within communities. With its current 150,000 registered traders and this constant flow of new traders, we assume an average trading fee per trader at 0.075% (making the fee calculation at 0.15% based on traded volume).

☞ COSS FSA (fee split allocation), where holders of the COSS token on a weekly basis (announced to be daily in COSS 2.0) get 50% of the trading fees accumulated on the exchange. The fees are paid out in the various tokens/coins they are collected in (regardless of value on the COSS token itself). So, per day will be the total amount of trading fees divided by 2 (50%), then divided by the amount of circulating COSS tokens (approx. 120M) multiplied against the amount of COSS tokens you hold.

Now to some mouthwatering assumptions with calculations.

☞ 2019: COSS average 50M USD per day in trading volume. Total anticipated trading volume for the year 18,250,000,000 USD.

☞ With an average trading fee of 0.15%, the total collected trading fee will be: 27,375,000 USD of which 50% represent 13,687,500 USD

☞ Now we divide this by the circulating supply of 120M and we get: 0.1140 USD per COSS token. This is an annual return of approximately 200% based on today's average trading value of 0.0549 USD.

☞ What would an average investor see as a good annual ROI? Should we go greedy and say 20% or basic and say 5–10%? Regardless, even at 20%, it shows that the COSS token is currently undervalued by 10x.

With these calculations we have not accounted for:
The COSS token appreciation if they meet the volume (could easily be 15–30 times today's price). The other tokens the FSA is paid out in (today's market is still very low).

Thus, I will be looking at increasing my portfolio to a minimum of 1M COSS (today's cost approx. 55,000 USD).

Tokens ⇅	Available
COSS	1000000.24716000

With an estimated 2019 return of 0.1140 USD per token, that will give me 114,000 USD annually without ever having to think about the COSS tokens trading price and without selling a single COSS token EVER.

Another bonus which is nothing less than pure gravy is the fact that the "daily" FSA also pays out COSS tokens based on all trading fees collected in COSS, so my portfolio will grow daily and only increase my annual return as we move forward.

Also note that the other 50% of the fees is COSS turnover, which is 13,687,000 USD, allowing them to have a monthly budget of over 2M for operations and marketing. This does not include added revenue from token listings, advisory fees, hosting of ICOs, and whatever COSS chooses to bring to the table.

So back to the original question. WILL IT HAPPEN? Of course, only time will tell, and you should never invest more than you can afford to lose. But I see big changes in how COSS is operating as a company and I have turned from being a bystander to becoming a strong supporter. But hey, that's just me 😉

 These issues of transience, gambles, and uncertainty over our options can all lead to some security fears about cryptocurrencies like Bitcoin.

With all those spikes and those competing platforms, how do we know where to turn? That is why we need a strong crypto-friendly banking system to help with regulations, standards, and general security. Right now, there is a lack of trust in crypto-banking, as well as a lack of respect. A crypto-friendly option would provide the means and trust to help investors get started. They could create a fairer system that may not be so biased towards those whales.

In fact, there are many reasons why crypto-friendly banks are vital to the future of cryptocurrency.

Gradually, decentralized trust will be accepted as a new and effective trust model. We have seen this evolution of understanding before - on the Internet.

—ANDREAS ANTONOPOULOS

Chapter 5

Why Crypto-Friendly Banks Are Vital To The Future Of Cryptocurrency

The world of Bitcoin is a confusing one for anyone new to this currency. Outsiders know that there are investors making profits with these cryptocurrencies and that many proclaim it to be the future of banking. However, conflicting views and policies create doubt. This is a legal tender, but only in certain countries, and there is no global regulator. It is no wonder that it has taken so long to create crypto-friendly banks.

The need for a more crypto-friendly banking system is clear when we consider the attitudes of many leading nations. There are concerns over the long-term value of Bitcoin and other currencies within much the EU, as well as the US, Canada, and Australia. Many nations are also worried about the security risks of this ICO system. China, Russia, Vietnam, and South Korea have banned ICOs altogether.

The obstacles between banks and cryptocurrency users are clear. There is:
a) a lack of trust in the system.
b) a lack of understanding of the technology involved.
c) a lack of respect for cryptocurrency users and investors.

Why are crypto-friendly banks so important for the future of this sector?

Crypto-friendly banks aren't the enemy here. In fact, they are the middle-ground solution between the old-fashioned banking system and modern Bitcoin options. Financial ministries don't trust the cryptocurrency system because of the lack of structure and regulation. The idea that Bitcoin would eradicate the need for banks scared them. A well-designed crypto-friendly bank should offer a compromise where everyone is satisfied. Yet, there is still lots of resistance.

Some countries are more open to the prospect of cryptocurrencies and crypto-banking than others. In fact, back in January, The Swiss Economics Minister stated that Switzerland wanted to be the "crypto-nation." This meant a more open, friendly attitude toward crypto-banking than that of other nations. Instead of focusing on security issues and the potentially volatile nature of these currencies, they want to invite investors and companies to Switzerland. Many start-ups have since based themselves in the country. Switzerland has the trust in the system, understanding of the technology, and the respect of users to make this work.

Banking start-ups offer solutions to those main problems in crypto-friendly banking.

There is clearly still plenty of uncertainty and hesitation when it comes to the bigger giants of the banking world. This is where smaller banking start-ups see their chance to strike and fill that gap in

the market. These new companies want to break the mold with a friendly approach. They can do so because they:
a) are prepared to put their trust in these cryptocurrencies where others back down.
b) are prepared to invest in the technology to provide an effective service.
c) are prepared to listen to users and investors and provide options to suit their needs.

These new banking businesses understand the popularity of Bitcoin and other cryptocurrency products with a younger market. The idea here is that not only can they cash in on a trend—while making traditional banks seem old-fashioned—they can also prove to be customer friendly. They want to provide more choices and investment options, securing the millennial banker and tomorrow's millionaires.

Whale watching becomes necessary.
Greater regulation and improved options for the everyday user is also vital when trying to combat all those whales in the cryptocurrency ocean. These whales are a massive influence on the market, with a small handful of users owning as much as 40%. Crashes and fluctuations are often the result of their trades. Therefore, wider adoption of cryptocurrency banking and accessibility for the average user could be an advantage. The more we can limit the influence of whales, the more stability there is in the system. The more stable the system, the better the chance of countries adopting it in the future.

Cryptocurrency users need a crypto-friendly bank—and they need it now.

There is no doubt that too many major banks and leading financial powers are a dead weight here. Their inability to see past the risks and embrace the innovations stalls any momentum for crypto-banking as a worldwide system. These new banking start-ups offer the solution for a friendlier, understanding system. Here users finally feel like they have a legitimate form of cryptocurrency and a chance to build on investments. These banks are a compromise between tradition and innovation. This is the best way for cryptocurrency to gain some stability and work towards mass adoption. Users just need more companies and countries to sign up.

 Security really is the biggest threat to the future of cryptocurrency—which is why we also need to consider the potential of STO tokenization.

Security Token Offerings are an alternative to the unregulated, insecure system of the Initial Coin Offering. These new tokens should provide a fully regulated share of assets in a manner that is fully compliant with the appropriate laws. This sense of transparency could then lift the crypto-banking world to new heights. Users would be free to take part knowing that they have a great safety net.

That is why we believe that STO Tokenization could shape the evolution of crypto-banking.

Many regulators are quick to apply existing compliance practices that treat tokens as a security, therefore elevating the barriers and costs of implementation for entrepreneurs.

—WILLIAM MOUGAYAR

Chapter 6

STO Tokenization Could Shape The Evolution Of Crypto-Banking

Cryptocurrency was once the future of banking for many investors. It was the radical, visionary approach that would make traditional banking obsolete. Today, crypto-banks are a little more mainstream, a little less radical, and in need of evolution. Issues with regulations and Initial Securities Offerings (ISOs) continue to slow the momentum of the industry. Many start-up creators and investors say it is time to embrace Security Token Offerings. They see this as a great new venture for improved private stock exchange experiences. Is this really the case? Or are ISOs here to stay?

The current problem with Initial Coin Offerings (ICOs) is the lack of security and regulation.
At the moment, cryptocurrency and crypto-banking are seen as risky ventures. The official line from major national regulators is still one of caution. Therefore, cryptocurrency can't attract those that aren't willing to risk big. The issues are simple:
a) there is no regulation to protect investors and no rights for shareholders,
b) there are security risks when it comes to trading,
c) the lack of transparency opens the door to scammers and lost capital,
d) it all seems a little old-fashioned for an evolving cryptocurrency.

When all these issues are laid out like this, it is no wonder that many cryptocurrency advocates champion a new approach. The only way for cryptocurrency to thrive and develop is to improve its appeal to investors.

Tokenization with STOs could be the answer.
These new security tokens could help transform the cryptocurrency industry into something much more appealing and accessible. These tokens offer the following:
a) a fully regulated share of the assets for improved protection,
b) a low-cost solution for easy access to capital, and
c) compliance with international laws on the same level as traditional banks.

Essentially, this is a way of bringing the best of both worlds together. Some cryptocurrency veterans may see it as a compromise, or even a step backward. Yet, there are hopes that this new approach could change crypto-banking for the better. Improved regulation lessens that sense of risk. Compliance with international and national laws could finally put crypto-banks and advisors on the same page. The end result here should be a greater acceptance of cryptocurrency as a legitimate player. There are still risks involved, like any investment. However, the security of the STO is just enough of a safety net.

There is still some debate over whether or not STOs are the future for cryptocurrencies.
Those that are used to the rebellious, alternative world of Bitcoin might not approve of these compromises. Some will argue that as long as ICOs remain compliant and trustworthy, there is no need for any major change. Then there are those concerned that the whales will overrun the system. These giants of cryptocurrency are sure to take advantage of this new tokenization, and the young investors they bring in.

Yet, there is also the idea that these new tokens could appeal to younger investors on the private stock exchange. As with all industries, crypto-banks need to appeal to the youth market. Any bank needs to stay relevant, regardless of the currency or methods. This improved security and wider access could open that door. Cautious newcomers could find these low-cost stock options, take a less-risky gamble, and see if it pays off. It all sounds like the perfect way for them to dip their toes in the water.

It is still early days in regard to these security tokens. Time will tell if they actually do draw in the young investors promised.
Crypto-banks have to evolve like everyone else. They need to prove that young investors have a chance to succeed. We have to remember that this isn't an entirely new concept. We can trace some of these ideas back to SAFT agreements. SAFT is a Simple Agreement for Future Tokens. Rather than seeing a complete shift into STOs from ICOs, it is more likely that we will see a divide. Established companies and new startups will have a choice between the tried-and-tested formula and this new approach.

There is an interesting article from **Forbes** earlier this year that makes a bold prediction about the future of STOs. They claim that if this was the year of "realizing the mistake of the utility token", then 2019 will be when we see the rise of tokenized securities. In other words, the coming year is a chance to rectify early mistakes made in the cryptocurrency industry and to spark that evolution into a more secure era. Security token offerings will come into their own in 2019, but at what price?

 Meanwhile, others are turning to the potential of the stablecoin as a new concept.

This new stablecoin is part of a collateralized system that should mean a strong pairing with liquid assets and improved regulations. Both Tether and Gemini have shown that there is potential here. Still, we can't overlook the additional costs, centralization issues and the lack of currencies involved. This is still one to watch. The ideas are appealing and there is the scope to take this global once companies are a little less single-minded about the dollar.

But does the stablecoin have a secured place in cryptocurrency right now?

Stablecoin stable?

But you have to build a network of important players that are also trusted to solve for the [sic] trust problem of a stablecoin.

—TYLER WINKLEVOSS

Chapter 7

Does The Stablecoin Have A Secured Place In Cryptocurrency Right Now?

Stablecoins are slowly creeping into the cryptocurrency market and the concept appears to be here to stay. There are some cryptocurrency enthusiasts and writers that herald the stablecoin as the future for secure, collateralized trading. *Forbes* even ran an article declaring it as "the holy grail of cryptocurrency." However, we have to wonder if some supporters are getting a little ahead of themselves. This "stable" option has potential, but is it really the perfect product that traders have been waiting for?

Stability is a word that will gain a lot of interest from traders and regulators.

One of the biggest issues with cryptocurrency is instability. Massive fluctuations in value hold the industry back. New investors walk away from the risk and regulators issue more warnings. Stability is the answer. The industry needs something with a more solid foundation to get past regulators and appeal to new investors, rather than just whales. But in what form? An unstable market surely needs a stable coin in order to regain a little balance and trust.

Supporters of the stable coin highlight the following benefits:
a) clear value via a collateralized system.
b) strong pairing with liquid assets and major currencies.
c) improved securities and regulations.

The idea here is that stablecoins offer this assurance by creating a value that is stable against an equivalent, more standard currency. There are new stablecoins tied to the dollar, euro, and other major currencies. The list is steadily growing, as more and more companies look to profit from this new solution. One well-known example that some traders have turned to is Tether. In fact, this is one of the top-performing cryptocurrencies for September 2018. Then there is the Gemini dollar, which is tied one-to-one with the dollar. Gemini, in particular, is a potential game changer because of the company's determination to improve compliance and surveillance programs.

Many companies are saying the right things about this collateralized system, but it has some issues right now. They include:
a) the expense to the trader.
b) disputes are the true links and value of the pairing.
c) problems with centralization.
d) the lack of currencies involved.

A dollar's worth of a questionable new stable coin costs an actual dollar.
That means risking a fully liquid asset for something unverified. This isn't so bad with small amounts, but are traders really willing to gamble larger amounts on this "stable" pairing? This raises additional

questions over the role of whales in all this. How will their vast shares of these new stablecoins impact fluctuations in value?

Stablecoin companies don't yet fit the profile of the transparent, decentralized provider that crypto-traders are after.

This is a major obstacle for all of these new companies and the future of stablecoins. Cryptocurrency users want DAOs. These decentralized autonomous organizations provide the systems and methods that users wanted when turning away from traditional approaches. More importantly, cryptocurrency users want a decentralized system with transparency and a sense of trust. Tether fails to provide that right now, especially after recent issues with the Paradise Papers. They are also a centralized system.

Then there is this focus on the dollar.
The all-mighty dollar is an important player in global finance, but crypto-banks can't develop via dollar trading alone. Many cryptocurrency advocates will try and sell the potential of the stable coin based on this pairing with the US dollar. There are a number of currencies tied to stablecoins right now, but not enough of them. Where do the Yen and the Pound fit into all of this? When we consider the current fear in China over cryptocurrency and its bans, we may not see Yuan links anytime soon either.

Can these stablecoins really offer the stability that crypto-banking needs right now?
The idea of the stablecoin is great in theory. There is no doubt that the cryptocurrency industry needs a little stability to evolve. Mass adoption of cryptocurrency across the world may be achievable with viable pairings. However, that stability isn't quite there yet. There are too many issues over validity and centralization for mass adoption right now. The lack of links with other major currencies is another stumbling block. As soon as transparent DAOs can offer a truly stable, secure product, the stablecoin may finally thrive.

 The stablecoin isn't the only factor with a security issue.

The ongoing concerns about security and banking regulations meant that the SEC failed to give the green light to a number of projects. Those in favor of these ETFs saw a familiar, regulated system that would finally bridge the gap between the "darker" side of cryptocurrency and the safety of regular banking. The February 27th, 2019 closing date for applications saw a turning of the tide. Those in charge were finally open to these new approaches and would welcome applications with a more open mind.

We were left asking, will February 27th be the turning point for Bitcoin ETFs?

Once Wall Street starts putting money into Bitcoin - we're talking about hundreds of millions, billions of dollars moving in - it's going to have a pretty dramatic effect on the price.

—BARRY SILBERT

Chapter 8

Will February 27th Be The Turning Point For Bitcoin ETFs?

The issue of Bitcoin exchange-traded funds (ETFs) seems to be stuck in a bit of a ditch right now. Applications are rejected, resubmitted, and then left in limbo as the US Securities and Exchange Commission (SEC) pushes back dates for reviews. Approvals for Bitcoin ETFs, regardless of the actual applicant involved, are sure to become a catalyst for the evolution of Bitcoin and crypto-markets. The problem at the moment is that there is still a level of uncertainty over these approvals. Which proposals will get the green light, if any? Will applicants finally break free and bring ETFs to the market?

Those in favor of Bitcoin exchange traded funds believe it is about time the SEC gave in.
The main aim here is to tempt more investors from the retail market. There are conflicting views about the need to bring in mainstream investors. Still, many see this as the only way to help legitimize Bitcoin and the cryptocurrency industry. ETF creators and supporters believe that this is the right approach because:
a) ETFs are familiar and comfortable, unlike many of the Bitcoin exchanges in operation at the moment.
b) ETFs would herald another stepping stone between the uncertain territory of current crypto-banking and the more recognizable systems of traditional banking.

The focus on this fight between Bitcoin ETF providers and regulators mostly centers around the US. The actions and rejections of the SEC mean that this side of the market has gained a lot of publicity. However, US Bitcoin users shouldn't overlook the fact that Sweden has worked with Bitcoin ETFs for years now. Unsurprisingly, the SEC halted US trading with these funds too. Countries like Sweden prove that it can be done. Yet, the SEC continues to resist.

Many applicants have tried, failed, and tried again.
There are many applications under review right now, many of which are appeals on previous rejections. The SEC rejected Bitcoin ETF applications from GraniteShares, ProShare, Direxion, and the Winklevoss brothers over the summer. Some of these companies are determined to reverse the decision. The SEC is looking at proposals from VanEck and SolidX, as well as a proposition from Coinbase. Coinbase is looking to develop an ETF with BlackRock, one of the biggest asset managers around.

What is the probability of approvals occurring this time around?
The answer here depends on how optimistic we are prepared to be. There is room for optimism because the SEC has softened its stance a little. The fact that previously rejected applicants have a second

chance at all is a start. The decision to bring public opinion into the review process is another step in the right direction. In fact, the SEC has received over 1,400 comments about the VanECk Solid X Bitcoin trust, so the interest is there. There is also promise in the form of a voice of support within the SEC. Commissioner Hestor Peirce has stated her approval of Bitcoin ETFs in the past, claiming that the current SEC stance is counterproductive. This voice, if influential on others, could prove useful in turning the tide.

However, we can't overlook the fact that the SEC keeps pushing back its dates for a final answer on approvals.
The deadline was, at one point, slated as November 5th. The SEC now has a deadline for 2019 on February 27th for the review of nine Bitcoin ETF proposals. There is still reluctance here, as key concerns remain at the forefront of the assessor's minds. SEC regulators will always cite security risks and the volatility of cryptocurrency as major reasons to hold back on approvals. One of the reasons that so many proposals failed this summer was the issue of market manipulation. There is the fear that a reliance on a single exchange puts users at risk of such manipulation. Those new mainstream investors could fall victim to whales. Still, if the market can remain stable for a while longer, this could work in its favor.

What does the future hold for Bitcoin ETFs?
This February 27th deadline comes just in time for the expected rollout of ICE's own Bitcoin ETF—Bakkt on January 24th. Bakkt could be a major player in the market, thanks to this collaboration between the Intercontinental Exchange, Starbucks, and Microsoft. If this Bitcoin ETF goes through, it could open the door to other applicants. This could be a big turning point, the moment where the Bitcoin ETF issue finally comes out of limbo and into public consciousness. Advocates, critics, and investors will await February 27th with great anticipation.

 So far, the future of cryptocurrency and the crypto-banking world has largely rested on the shoulders of Bitcoin and those that trade with it.

As we mentioned before, Bitcoin remains the leader of the pack and the household name. Still, there is a fight going on between its closest rivals. This includes Ethereum and Ripple. Ethereum has been second best for a long time—commonly used but not at the top. However, recent declines and departing traders have leveled the playing field, allowing Ripple to close in and overtake its position. These contenders are experiencing the same spikes and crashes as Bitcoin. This proves that not only is this a volatile market, it really is anyone's game.

So, is Ethereum's place in the cryptocurrency ecosystem secure?

 **ETH 2019**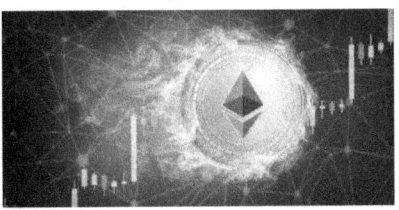

> When I came up with Ethereum, my first first thought was, 'Okay, this thing is too good to be true.' As it turned out, the core Ethereum idea was good - fundamentally, completely sound.
>
> —VITALIK BUTERIN

Chapter 9

Is Ethereum's Place In the Cryptocurrency Ecosystem Secure?

To say that Ethereum is struggling at the moment is a bit of an understatement. A report on its status from December 7, 2018, states that the ETH price declined so sharply that it fell to 19-month lows just over $80 and was down 94% from its January peak against USD. The golden child of the cryptocurrency world has grown up and not met expectations. The current situation is concerning for those involved, especially with Ripple snapping at their heels. So is this a major downturn with no solution, or just a bump in the road?

Where are things going wrong for Ethereum?
To be honest, users have experienced a number of issues with ETH for a while now. Recent price declines just made the problem more visible. These problems include:

a) issues with low speeds,
b) high prices,
c) security issues over access and use of the system,
d) and key players exiting entirely.

Basically, there was a perfect storm of issues. Users struggled with the slow processes and costs and generally became frustrated. This discontent spread over social media and forums, adding more negative publicity. Further issues of a network takeover and the departure of Tron and EOS worsened the issue. Large whales have also made massive transfers in recent months, disrupting the market further. Bring these all together and there is no real surprise that ETH declined so much.

This is a big concern for the cryptocurrency world.

Ethereum should be a major player and indeed has been BTC's closest rival for a long time. There are major ICOs using ETH right now, including Stream41, Realcasino, Ryfts, Enzym, and more. Many grabbed hold of the system when it first emerged because it seemed so promising. It had:
a) the design,
b) a focus on decentralization,
c) the ability to reinvest with ease.

Cryptocurrency users need choice and stable options across the market for the industry to thrive.
But if the world's #3 cryptocurrency goes through this many problems, it reflects poorly on the industry more generally. This was a venture meant to change the landscape in a positive way. Many celebrated the creators—Vitalik Buterin, Justin Drake, and Karl Floresch—for their attempts to address issues with the current system. Buterin wanted this to be a positive change for the ecosystem, with great stability. Clearly, that wasn't to be the case.

We can't forget that it was only this summer that many users and publications proclaimed Ethereum to be the "future" of blockchain and an important part of the cryptocurrency industry. It was popular for the reasons above and gained interest over 2018, with a significant increase in developers. Tron and EOS were part of a much wider group of users, including NEO, Cardano, Stellar, Qtuma, and ICON. Even Amazon's own blockchain partnership was with ETH.

Ethereum's place in the crypto-ecosystem is under threat.
This dramatic shift in fortunes means that there are big problems if Ethereum is to maintain its position as a contender to Bitcoin's throne. Back in June, Medium.com writer Michael Spencer wrote: "If Bitcoin is shrouded in controversy, Ethereum is bathed in possibility." It is impressive the difference that six months can make. While Bitcoin isn't without its issues, the future prospects for Ethereum appear far less rosy when we consider current events.

We must also remember that the fight for supremacy in cryptocurrency isn't just between ETH and BTC.
There is a battle for 2nd place here against Ripple. Reports from October 13th suggest that Ripple is in contention to take over more permanently. Ripple saw a steady price rise of 115% in the 3rd week of September. This may not be a permanent shift in position, but it is significant at a time where other options struggle. There is still the chance that Ripple too could fall foul the volatile market and, by that logic, we shouldn't rule out a possible comeback for Ethereum either.

So, what does the future really hold for Ethereum?
Perhaps we shouldn't be so quick to give up on ETH. Despite all these issues and the major crashes, there is some light at the end of the tunnel. It has been reported that Ethereum, alongside Litecoin, may become part of the US futures market. The notion is that ErisX will begin offering spot trading in early 2019, and then more established futures trading later that year. This would open the currency up to new investments. This could be the life raft that Ethereum needs. It may even help it to push Ripple aside again and

maintain that #2 spot. It has been a rollercoaster year for Ethereum in 2018. 2019 looks set to be no different.

 The chapter above shows the uncertainty for Ethereum.

There are also questions over whether token swaps could help to improve Ethereum's position in the ranking in the long run or make things worse. An increase in token swaps could see traders and big whales shifting large quantities of one currency for something more trendy. As Ethereum is the entry-level product for more ICOs, this could mean a lot of traders ditching this currency in favor of something "better." The worst-case scenario here is that the industry gives up on Ethereum so hard that it crashes spectacularly.

Still, there is also the chance that competitors could see similar losses. What is the status of token swaps in the evolution of cryptocurrency?

Binance supports permanent #TRX main net swap and $TRX/USDT trading pairs now.

—JUSTIN SUN @JUSTINSUNTRON

Chapter 10

Token Swaps In The Evolution Of Cryptocurrency

Many traders will agree that we can't have a true cryptocurrency exchange without an effective, secure token swap system. Token swaps provide the chance to switch out tokens from one blockchain for another. The idea here is that it allows a trader to improve their investments, while also allowing new companies to thrive in the industry. The question is, what does this evolution mean for currencies like Ethereum? Will token migration and a change of direction by new ICOs send ETH deeper into its downward spiral?

The basic principle behind the token swap is nothing new.
There are often swaps in traditional banking as one form of currency replaces another. There are many reasons for this:
a) outdated coins are replaced by a new version.

b) new denominations occur and need to be brought into the chain.
c) banknotes require new security measures.

However, it is a slightly different game when it comes to cryptocurrency. The ratios remain the same. One unit of the new, desirable currency is equal to that of the old, undesirable one—one dollar's worth from one form in exchange for a dollar's worth of another. There is also that same sense of replacing the obsolete with something more relevant.

The difference is that the currency isn't always like for like.
Users can swap new currency units for old ones at the same rate. If we want a good example of this, there are no better places to turn than to Tron and EOS—two of 2018's major players. These companies began life on Ethereum and ERC20 tokens—as many startups do. As they progressed and grew, they switched focus to their own blockchain and a stronger identity. It was then time to swap out the Ethereum for their own tokens and cement their brand, which meant a 1:1 token swap.

Goodbye Ethereum and hello shiny new stablecoins?
This raises some questions over the role of ETH and other leading cryptocurrencies if these token swaps become more common. With Tron and EOS, ETH was
little more than the entry-level product—a stepping stone to bigger and better things. Token exchanges allow investors to discard their ETH, or other currencies, and enjoy the trendiest tokens from these new providers. And when we say discard, we are being literal. All the unwanted ERC20 token EOS and Tron received in these swaps were burned.

So what does this mean for ETH, which is already having a pretty turbulent year?
This may have a negative influence on the presence of Ethereum, which is already struggling in a fight for 2nd place against Ripple. Tron and EOS aren't alone in this mass migration away from

Ethereum. ICON, Augur, Zilliqa, and many more have shifted to their own blockchains, or are in the process of doing so. Ethereum seems less like the heir to the crypto-throne and more like a charity bled dry by its beneficiaries.

Still, there is the potential for many cryptocurrency veterans to see a similar fate.
At this point, it is also important to look at the place of Tether in this situation. On October 19th, it was reported that Tether experienced an outflow of $610 million in October. Meanwhile, no new tokens have entered circulation since September 21st. One contributing factor here could be the amount of token swaps. Major players and whales are swapping vast amounts of USDT for new stablecoins from start-ups like Gemini and Paxos.

Atomic swaps increase the appeal and ease of use for users.
There was a point where these swaps felt a little risky. Traders could send large sums of money to exchanges and receive nothing in return —another gamble in the volatile cryptocurrency world. Atomic swaps offer a bigger guarantee. Both sides have to fulfill their end of the arrangement or the whole deal is off. Therefore, atomic swaps are far safer and more appealing than their name suggests. This safety net will only encourage more traders to swap their ETH coins for something "better."

It is all about out with the old and in with the new when it comes to these token swaps.
There is no doubt that an increase in token swap platforms and apps can only help new companies pursue their own blockchain ventures. Atomic swaps will add security to the process and help traders swap their ETH or USDT for something new and exciting. Therefore, token swaps are sure to play a big role in the evolution and future of the industry. Evolution means survival of the fittest, so time will tell where Ethereum fits in.

 All in all, it hasn't been the best year for cryptocurrencies and developing ICOs.

Many new ICOs have died off before they could really get going. The increased volatility of currencies and concerns over regulations in ETFs haven't helped. This uncertainty shows why it is so important that all ICOs have an endgame. At the moment, many newcomers fail to think ahead and see the bigger picture. They lack the business skills and brand identity to proceed, while also expressing a clear lack of understanding of the market. This is a business, so it needs to have a clear business plan. It needs a brilliant white paper not dissimilar from those we mentioned before. What is the end goal for the currency? Are there plans to develop into an IPO?

This is why it is vital for ICOs to have an endgame.

ICOs are obviously a new and interesting form of funding for blockchain-based protocols, but it's not clear that all of them comply with U.S. securities laws or that all of them are companies that have good native use cases for new coins.

—NAVAL RAVIKANT

Chapter 11

Why It Is Vital For ICOs To Have An Endgame

At the end of December 2017, Coindesk ran an article full of predictions from Ripple's chief technical officer. Among those predictions was the idea that 2018 was to be the "year of the great ICO hangover." The bubble would burst and ICOs would die off. While 2018 isn't quite over yet, recent downward trends and the deaths of countless ICOs suggest that this wasn't too far-fetched. There are fewer ICOs in operation now than during the summer. Furthermore, many ICOs fail to live longer than 5 months. Is this all purely down to a lack of long-term planning? Did these failed operations even have an endgame?

There is a high mortality rate for ICOs, and this isn't a temporary blip either.

A study from Boston College found that just 44.2% of token projects remain active in their fifth month. The numbers of ICOs in the market have fallen steadily in the latter half of this year. There are a few areas where we can assign some blame. They include:
a) a lack of value in the current market.
b) poor brand identity.
c) poor money management
d) a lack of reporting

What we see here are many start-ups from young, enthusiastic entrepreneurs with no real vision. It is no wonder that these projects fail in the fifth month—there wasn't a long-term plan to manage the ICO at that point. Newcomers go in big at the start, drawing people in with concepts and great exchanges. The figures and forecasts look great for the short term, but there is no business or financial plan for what is to come.

Simply put, many start-ups lack the skilled personnel to create something of worth.
They don't have the consumer relation skills to understand the perfect niche that they should occupy. They don't have the branding skills to market themselves properly. They certainly don't have the financial skills to manage the product like a true ICO. A lack of identity and mainnet presence means no way of progressing with crypto exchanges and product development.

This is why ICO investment is such a gamble for new users.

A secure investment requires a sense of confidence in the new system.
Investors need to know that this is a reliable, forward-thinking company that will have a big impact on the market. This means some idea of the business plan and long-term goals of the team. There should be some idea of the aims for the development of the currency in order for it to remain valuable. Yet, many fail to look

beyond the launch date and the dollar signs as they raise their funds.

Of course, that is if there is even a short-term plan. We can't ignore the fact that the endgame here for many ICO startups is simply to scam users as quickly and quietly as possible. These frauds come and go just as easily as those that may genuinely want to succeed.

For every success story, there is also a failure.

Many ICOs come and go in the blink of an eye.
The next big thing forecast for the start of December could be dead in the water by 2019. Many that saw early success back in the highs of August are no longer with us. A great example of a failure is Telegram's TON—the telegram open network. They raised $1.7 billion to develop the system, with no timeline or long-term plan on releasing it on exchanges. It was shortsighted from the start. If there was an endgame, it was a closely-guarded secret.

But there are clearly exceptions to the rule, such as Tron and EOS.
These ICOs are performing well. In fact, these, and a handful of other top names are expected to outperform leading cryptocurrency giants in coming weeks. These ICOs have a strong mainnet presence and now embrace token swaps for improved trading. Their switch to a new, personal blockchain gives them an improved brand identity that helps separate them from ETH. This brings the big whales and big trades into the equation. It is easy to suspect that this was all part of the endgame plan. The smart moves and gradual growth of these companies show the forward thinking lacking in most start-ups.

Of course, the endgame can always change as new ideas and proposals come along.
ICOs need to be able to adapt and adjust these business plans to enhance their chance of longevity. For example, some may develop aspirations of creating an IPO. Bitmain worked hard with a clear

financing plan to do just that in September. This means real-time value and clear shares in the market.

This all shows that an endgame really is essential to succeed in the cryptocurrency world.
A mass extinction of ICOs isn't necessarily in the cards anytime soon. There will always be those that decide to test out the market—either as a legitimate venture or a scam. Many will continue to experience the same early deaths for the same simple reasons. Yet, there are those exceptions to the rule that show that it is possible to find a market with great crypto exchanges. That they can build something strong, stable, appealing, and profitable. It is all about that endgame. If ICOs don't have one in mind, they won't succeed.

 Endgames are essential in turbulent times.

2018 may have been rough for the future of cryptocurrency, but there is a pretty strong shaft of light at the end of that tunnel. This largely comes from the potential of other investors across the world. There are a few countries and regions that are veterans when it comes to ICO development and trading—such the US and Central Europe. Others, such as China, are much further behind. Yet, China is showing an interest. Their Center for Information and Industry Development sees crypto-banking as a place for development. Their outright ban of cryptocurrencies has also softened, with new allowances for Bitcoin ownership on domestic soil.

China's growing role in the cryptocurrency market cannot be denied.

China just banned ICO fundraising. They did Silicon Valley and the U.S. a favor - now we get first dibs.

—ADAM DRAPER

Chapter 12

China's Growing Role In The Cryptocurrency Market

China's Center for Information and Industry Development (CCID) has just compiled its most recent list of the most interesting and top-ranking cryptocurrency projects. This ranking project began in May and appears to be a consistent attempt for the CCID to keep up with trends. This system raises some interesting questions for those following the global development of cryptocurrency and its leading players. Is China ready to make a major play as it loosens some of its crypto-laws? If so, who stands to win or lose?

The fact that there is an updated rankings list at all is interesting because of the status of cryptocurrency in China.

Until very recently, there has been an outright ban on cryptocurrency across the country.
Some would say that this is due to a fear of the industry and security risks. Others cite deeper political issues and concerns of a global

market on domestic finances. On October 26th, the Shenzhen Court of International Arbitration confirmed that it is now legal to own Bitcoin—and other cryptocurrencies—as long as the investments are on Chinese ground. This doesn't change the outright ban on trading and ICOs, but it is a step in the right direction for a Chinese cryptocurrency market.

These updated rankings place leading figures in questionable positions.

What is more interesting here is the placement of some of the leading figures in the cryptocurrency world. Bitcoin has long held the top spot as the best performing and most trusted option in western markets. Its longevity, security, and familiarity mean that it consistently remains ahead of its closest rivals—such as Ethereum and Ripple.

In December, the CCID placed it in 18th place. The top three right now are EOS, Ethereum, and GXchain. Another interesting factor here is the emphasis on GXchain as a Chinese domestic project in the form of data economy. So what this means is that just as Bitcoin is heralded as a safe, legal option in a court of law, it slides down the ranks and becomes less appealing.

Why should we be concerned by this if China isn't a major player in cryptocurrency right now?

Why does this all matter?
The answer is that it matters because of China's place in the global financial stage. If they were to lift a ban, allow for trading and encourage new ICOs, this could change the face of the industry. If China were to trade in Ethereum and reject Bitcoin in accordance with these rankings, the global rankings and prices could shift considerably. Chinese whales could dominate the market in whole new ways. At the moment, Ethereum is in a bit of a battle for

supremacy with the evolving Ripple. This interest from China could nudge their rival off.

We also can't overlook that fact that Chinese activity has already had an influence on the global markets.

A ban on ICOs and trading doesn't mean a complete lack of activity. There are start-ups that try to get through the gaps—either as scams or legitimate venture. A decline in P2P lending in 2015 hit the industry hard. Now it appears that interest here is on the rise. There are also a number of platforms that have relocated outside of China but still service Chinese users. Finally, there are some major players in China have some serious plans for Blockchain tech:

a) Bank of China is looking to invest in blockchain technology.
b) The Chinese Communist Party is openly talking about the pros and cons of blockchain investments.
c) The People's Bank of China has gone even further, with 68 patent applications within blockchain in 2017 alone.
d) They were followed by Alibaba, with 43 patents.

On that note, we should mention the start-up fundraiser for the Alibabacoin. Alibaba is not a big fan of Bitcoin, and their company owner is skeptical of cryptocurrency. As a result, they are keen to insist that the new Alibabacoin token has nothing to do with them. They claim that this is nothing more than a scam to deceive the public.

China's new rankings do matter, and so does any new decision still to come.

It would be naïve to think that the cryptocurrency world is run by the few countries that legalize and regulate the market. The majority of ICOs may come from the US, UK, and Central Europe, but there are traders and influential figures across the world. China may not have the platforms or traders on the same scale, but their actions now could direct the flow of traffic in 2019 and beyond.

 China is a leading force, but it is not alone.

Elsewhere, Singapore has thrown its hat into the ring with a new partnership with Binance. Binance recently saw success in Uganda, bringing crypto-trading to a whole new audience. Singapore was seen as an ideal new territory due to their deep pool of whales and other investors, the ICO developers based there, and the economic links to the Government. Singapore could help to strengthen the position of Binance —and cryptocurrencies more generally—in this Eastern sector. This expansion can only herald good prospects for the industry in 2019.

So, what is the potential significance of Binance Singapore?

2017 Sept: BTC price $3000, FUD / negative news abound.
3 months later: BTC price $20,000.

—CHANGPENG ZHAO @CZ_BINANCE

Chapter 13

The Potential Significance Of Binance Singapore

Binance is a platform that is expanding globally as it tries to take advantage of new interest and opportunities. For example, Binance Uganda recently began trading and brought 40,000 users on board in the first week alone. It seems like the company is testing the waters in new areas. One area of particular interest in Singapore and Southeast Asia more generally. Recent deals and developments show that a marriage of Binance and Singapore could be a match made in heaven. But, why is this deal so important and what might this mean for leading cryptocurrencies.

Binance Singapore is ready to help local traders.

Vertex Ventures investing in Binance to create a strong domestic exchange for fiat-to-cryptocurrency.

Binance is fairly new, just a year old. But a year can be a very long time in the crypto game. Countless deals are made and ICOs lost in that time. The landscape can alter greatly. Binance's own fortunes have been rocky, with issues in Japan, Hong Kong, and New York. However, the Uganda deal shows their initiative and Singapore is arguably the hottest market in cryptocurrency right now. Binance has also made a positive impression in Asia with a recent donation of Bitcoin and Ethereum for Japanese flood relief.

Why Singapore?
Before we consider this new Vertex Ventures proposal further, we need to understand the importance of Singapore in the current ecosystem. Singapore has:
a) A hungry new group of investors, including some potentially gigantic Southeast Asian whales.
b) Plenty of ICO creators looking to make the most of the current situation.
c) A strong connection between cryptocurrency providers and everyday traders.
d) Deep ties and regulations that go back to the government.
Singapore is seen as one of the hottest cities in the world right now for cryptocurrency investments and start-ups. There is a strong foundation in place already. The guidelines brought in a year ago have made cryptocurrency more interesting and accessible to investors in Singapore. The Monetary Authority of Singapore created a Guide to Digital Token Offering on security and utility tokens. Not only does this allow for greater transparency in the industry, but it also opens the doors to new users. In fact, this idea has led to a vast increase in ICOs in the country.

Meanwhile, ImToken—one of the region's leading Ethereum wallets—has relocated there from China.

Just in the last quarter of 2018—on October 31st—Bizkey launched "Token Day" in celebration of Bitcoin's 10th birthday. The aim here was to raise public awareness about the cryptocurrency world and entice new investors. Current investors can use their currency in stores in Singapore's Chinatown district for a good exchange rate. This is set to continue until November 18th. Binance Singapore could prove to be an important stepping stone for the development of cryptocurrencies in Southeast Asia.

There are a couple of eye-catching elements to this announcement about the future of Binance in Singapore.
The first is that Vertex Venture is actually operated by the local government, which puts a different emphasis on the approach. This is not simply some independent operation looking to cash in on the new craze. Singapore's officials want to create a transparent, clear, and accessible platform for trading in local currency. This local exchange should, therefore, work within the guidelines and safety nets already put in place. There is also talk of additional services in Southeast Asia and the ongoing development of Binance in the region.

In a way, this deal is very similar to Vertex Ventures into Grab.

This is where we get the second interesting part of this announcement.
This is a joint investment between Vertex Ventures Southeast Asia & India and another branch of Vertex Ventures China. Therefore, China has its foot in the door with this new option. There is a good chance that all notions of expansion relate to the former side of the company. Still, Chinese opinions on cryptocurrency are adjusting. Their new ranking systems and loosened laws mean that while some companies and ICOs once jumped ship to Singapore, others may soon head back the other way.

What could this all mean for leading cryptocurrencies?
Recent changes in Chinese rankings and issues with the Ethereum price mean that there are some questions over the place of the big three currencies in this market. Bitcoin isn't the golden child in some Eastern markets. Ethereum appears to have a stronghold in

Singapore with these links to Binance and leading wallets. Meanwhile, Ripple is still an area of interest for new investors. Ongoing development in Southeast Asia, sparked by Binance Singapore, could cause a shift in the landscape.

 This sense of hope for 2019 brings us back to the idea of the IPO.

These initial public offerings are a great way for 2018's best performing ICOs to expand their presence and connect with a new audience. This business venture could be profitable for all concerned, while also proving to be an annoyance for all those whales taking up far too much room. These new IPOs could help with those issues of transparency and regulation mentioned previously. There is less need to be scared of the risks with these public, regulated approaches.

So, which crypto companies are pushing forward towards IPO?

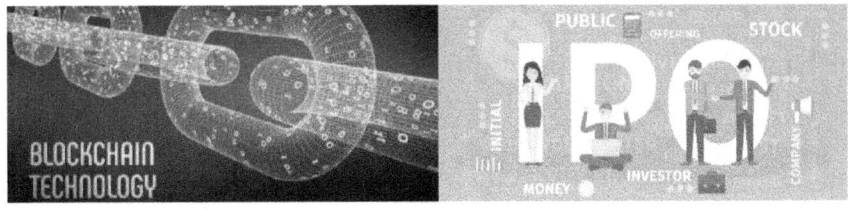

A token like ethereum has gone up 10 times faster than bitcoin, and it's fueling an ICO bubble no different then the dot-com IPOs of the late '90s.

—TONE VAYS

Chapter 14

Which Crypto Companies Are Pushing Forward Towards IPO?

Initial public offerings are something that many in the cryptocurrency market have talked about, but there has been little action. Some companies see the potential in going public in this manner. But there are also many more in no position to do so. So why should companies take this leap into IPO, and which companies can actually stand to benefit from this option?

Why is IPO so attractive to these crypto market leaders?

There are some in the crypto-world that see potential dangers in toying with IPO. These systems require companies to deal with a lot more red tape on regulations, which can be time-consuming and frustrating. They also require a greater level of transparency in the public eye. There is also the fact that this traditional approach steers companies away from the roots of ICOs and aims of decentralization. There are comfortable, fat whales out there that might not like this change.

However, there is a flip side to this that can benefit investors. IPO can:
a) draw in clients and traders currently put off by the cryptocurrency world.
b) bring in new regulations and greater cooperation with leading agencies.
c) create that safer, transparent system lacking in the risky world of cryptocurrency.

Essentially, this creates a more appealing, secure midway point between traditional banking and cryptocurrency trading. Cryptocurrency becomes accessible without the same risk. The mere promise of regulation is enough for new traders convinced that the crypto-world is full of high stakes gambles and con men. At the moment, these ideas a little more than hopes and dreams for some companies. This is the next step in a bigger plan.

Why haven't we seen cryptocurrency IPO yet?
The shift in focus and regulatory steps are a downside here. There is also the problem that it takes a lot of foresight and planning to create a company that can
evolve into an IPO. This is a progression for companies that already have strong placement in the market and want to build the brand in a more traditional playing field. It is for someone with a strong enough business plan and presence. This is one of the reasons why so few companies have made that leap. Either they didn't have that long-term plan in place, or they failed to get close to a point where IPO was an option. We can't forget that new platforms come and go in the blink of an eye. The lucky few with longevity may be able to progress.

Who are some of the major players in this evolution of cryptocurrency?
At the moment, there are three important names to keep in mind here. They are:
a) Epoch Partners Limited
b) Bitfury
c) Coinbase

Epoch Partners Limited has filed their motion for what is set to be a cryptocurrency-related IPO. They did so via the Japanese Financial Services Agency in September and promise a cap of 100b yen (or $900m). A partner of the company cited the rise of digital assets in investment portfolios as a cause for interest.

The more catchily named Bitfury has also stated interest in moving into IPO territory in the next couple of years. Japan isn't the intended target this time. Instead, their sights are set on Amsterdam, London, and Hong Kong.

Finally, there is Coinbase. This name should come as no surprise to those following the company's fortunes. There has been speculation over an announcement for a while now. On October 30th it was announced that there are plans to take Coinbase public in the future. The company is certainly in a good position to do so, with a new license from the New York Department of Financial Services.

Naturally, there are plenty of rumors flying around about the intentions of other companies. For example, there is some speculation of a venture by Bitmain. The IPO seems to be the logical next step for companies in a financially secure enough position to take it. Those that have the monetary backing, consumer interest, and secure regulations could improve their status in coming years or even months.

2019 could be the year that the cryptocurrency IPO becomes a reality. These public offerings could bridge the gap between the industries like never before.

 Increased use of IPOs and regulation across the world will help to smooth things out and bring in new traders.

The problem comes from an emerging threat—unauthorized crypto-mining within crypto-exchanges. There was a time when a little light mining was all fun and legal. Today, there is a criminal element using malware to target the laptops of unsuspecting people. It is such a problem that some exchanges are removing companies with links to mining.

Let's take a closer look at the growing threat of unauthorized crypto-mining in crypto-exchanges.

Mining in Crypto Exchanges

> We set up a small bitcoin and ethereum mining operation... that miraculously now is actually making a lot of money.
>
> —ABIGAIL JOHNSON

Chapter 15

The Growing Threat Of Unauthorized Crypto-Mining In Crypto-Exchanges

There was a time when crypto-mining sounded like a great option for those with the tools to succeed. If the market was right, there was the potential for some profit. The problem is that unauthorized crypto-mining is taking over and placing the reputation of the industry at risk.

The role of crypto-mining in cryptocurrencies.

So what is crypto-mining? At its heart, it is a chance to earn some extra cryptocurrency by cracking some algorithms via a computer. This is a popular idea because it is so accessible to anyone with the technology and the skill to earn. There are a number of crypto-mining pools that are highly popular, such as AntPool and Slush Pool —most of which work via Bitcoin. Whales can use these tools and market data to increase their always massive slice of the pie. However, ongoing threats mean that some exchanges have shut down ties with those that offer mining.

The biggest threat here is the criminal element behind secret, illegal, and unauthorized mining endeavors.

There is a scary chain of events that can happen here.
1) Smart miners find a way to break codes on other devices.
2) Crypto-mining attacks become more intense, with the use of malware and other security issues.
3) A skilled criminal sector starts scaling up the attacks and mining significant values.

One of the biggest concerns here is the use of malware to target devices and mine for currencies. Recent data from Malwarebytes shows that almost 200,000 computers in Australia alone were hit with malware this year. Miners sent it out, attack the device, and try and cash in on current price rises in the particular currency. Essentially, the attackers' software gets to work through unsafe sites while unsuspecting users browse the net.

The good news here is that the threat does tend to fluctuate just as wildly as the prices of the currencies.
As soon as a price drops, the attackers lose interest. There is also the fact that companies are wiser to the risks, and so are officials. The downside is that this may push the criminals in another direction. There are fears that mining attacks may migrate to the cloud, where they are harder to detect.

There is also a class action lawsuit underway against Bitmain—one of the largest, global cryptocurrency providers.
The claim here is that the company used unauthorized crypto-mining for its own benefit. This is where we go back to those legal customer

resources mentioned above. While some people will use legitimate mining tools in a responsible manner, it is clearly too easy to manipulate the system. Bitmain has been accused of using customer resources to mine for currencies before they become fully active. There are concerns that initial teething problems are actually signs that Bitmain was up to no good.

With all these risks, it is understandable that crypto-exchanges would want to distance themselves with companies that enable crypto-mining.
BTCC in Hong Kong has also severed its ties with any operations and members involved in mining. All mining servers in the BTCC Pool ceased operations on November 30, 2018, and there seems to be no aim to bring them back in the near future. The company says that this was due to little more than business adjustments. Yet, there are many that see the dangers in crypto-mining and want to distance themselves as much as possible.

Some are a little more transparent than others with their approaches.
CoinMarketCap is an exchange that cryptocurrency users need to keep an eye on. The company claims to be completely transparent and have made changes in recent months to level the playing field. This means removing volume requirements for exchanges and promoting equality. Yet, many of the top traders in their ranks now use "transaction" mining to get ahead. There are also concerns from users that CoinMarketCap may be keen on a little mining themselves.

This is a difficult issue and it hard to know where exchanges and providers stand.
The last thing that law-abiding cryptocurrency investors need is the fear that other traders and major companies may mine through their laptops. It is enough to make us all paranoid whenever our devices feel a little hotter or slower than normal. There are some agencies and exchange that understand the need for a fair, transparent system.

Some seem to be taking the right step to limit the impact of unauthorized mining. Others aren't really taking it that seriously at all.

 With all these pros and cons to the crypto-banking world, and such uncertainty with cryptocurrencies, it is important to understand the ICO public sale.

These sales are where newcomers and followers get to play their part and take home their fair share. This is where everything that you have learned about the cryptocurrency world comes into practice. Now that you know the difference between the main currencies, you need to get some into your personal wallet. Once you find the right ICO to invest in, you need to be aware of the right pre-sales and public sales. You need to be ready to hit the market and beat the whales at their own game.

Let's take a closer look at how to participate in an ICO public sale.

Initial Token Offering Public Sale
12 December 2018 @ 6pm GMT+8

Just because you call something a blockchain or an ICO, that doesn't mean you aren't subject to normal laws.

—JUAN BENET

Chapter 16

How To Participate In An ICO Public Sale?

The idea of taking part in an ICO public sale can be both daunting and exciting for those that are new to the world of cryptocurrencies and trading. There is often the notion that this vast crypto-ecosystem is dominated by whales that get all the money and all the best trades. There are whales that will take advantage of a new ICO sale and try and exert their dominance. Yet, there is still a place for the little guy —that is if they know where to begin. If you take the right first steps now, you can thrive in this world.

How do you get started?

The good news is that it is actually quite easy to take part in one of these public sales. All you need to do is:
a) acquire your cryptocurrency,

b) keep it all nice and safe in your blockchain wallet,
c) participate in the ICO sale,
d) secure your new tokens.

Getting your cryptocurrency:
The first thing to do is to make sure that you have the funds in place to buy into those public sales. This means stocking up on your currency of choice by making an exchange in fiat currency. Many newcomers will turn to Bitcoin or Ethereum as they are the most commonly used. However, you do need to take some time to research your currencies and the online exchanges to purchase them from.

Setting up a wallet:
All those new tokens need a safe home where they can be stored ready for your next trade. A cryptocurrency wallet is an online storage system that comes in three different types. They are software, hardware, and paper. Again, it helps to research the different options and suppliers to find a solution that works for you.

Participating in the ICO sale:
Once you have your funds set up in your secure wallet, you are free to use them in whatever ICO public sale that you want. Join up with the site, send over your currency, and receive the tokens of your choice. It helps to read up on the rules and limitations of each ICO sale. Some will have a small waiting period for the tokens. Others will make them available right away. You can choose to participate at either an initial exchange offering or the website of the ICO. The IEO is possibly the better choice because it provides a little more transparency about the deal and peace of mind for new users.

Securing the tokens in your wallet:
The transfer of the tokens isn't the final step here. You may have ownership of them via fair, legitimate trade, but you still need to make them secure. Make sure to transfer them into your wallet so you don't lose any of tokens.

Other important considerations to make when taking part in an ICO public sale.

This short guide makes the whole process sound quite simple. There are a number of steps to take, and there is quite a bit of research needed, but it becomes fairly easy once you have your initial fiat exchange and a new wallet. Still, there are additional considerations that you need to know before starting out.

The first is the issue of passing the KYC.

KYC means Know Your Customer. It is a security tool that means that only those with the right credentials, and that meet basic KYC requirements, can take part in Bitcoin exchanges or start an ICO. Compliance means greater transparency and trust. It may also make things easier in the long-run. Then there is the issue of pre-sales and crowd sales. There are lots of different names for different types of sale. This can be a little confusing for those starting out. There is a pre-sale before the main crowdfunding sale that helps ICOs raise a little more money. Some use this as a test run before the main event. Some also provide the coins at a better rate with other added perks. Again, research is vital.

Get started today to ensure that you don't miss out.

There are new ICOs that come onto the market all the time. This means lots of pre-sales, public sales, and all kinds of potential transactions. Traders and investors that are smart can choose the best platform, currencies, and companies to make a great trade. If you can get yourself set up on those first steps today, you are ready to go when the next sale launches. Get started with a wallet containing the currency of your choice. Read up on ICOs, different sales, and other options. Find out more about KYC requirement. The more you prepare for now, the easier it is to beat the whales at their own game. Don't be afraid to take that first step today.

 These public sales are a great tool, but they are not the only way into this world.

Another top opportunity for new investors is the Initial Exchange Offering. These systems act as a secure middleman between projects and contributors. This is a popular idea with many new users because of that increased sense of security and transparency. This system is also much fairer as it treats the less experienced as equal to those that have been in the game for a long time. Many also approve of this approach because it offers that familiarity of a "normal" banking system.

So let's explore the growing popularity and worth of the Initial Exchange Offering.

> Digital assets, including bitcoin, could save small businesses substantial transaction fees and provide an added layer of security to their payment processing.
>
> —PERIANNE BORING

Chapter 17

The Growing Popularity And Worth Of The Initial Exchange Offering

The Initial Exchange Offering is a new approach to crypto-banking that is slowly catching the interest of ICOs and traders across the world. This new system provides a different type of exchange where the exchange acts as middleman between projects and contributors. Currency is sent to an account on the site and distributed appropriately. Is this approach a good idea for ICOs and traders? Many in the crypto-world see the potential in this system and encourage others to get on board.

So why should we be so excited about these Initial Exchange Offerings when they sound like they could be a little more restrictive?

This two-way system brings a sense of control to proceedings that is essential in a number of ways. This new IEOs can offer the following:
a) greater security for users,
b) improved transparency compared to previous approaches,
c) a fairer system that can benefit those that are new to the game,
d) the sense that this is a reliable banking system.

Security:
Security is already a massive issue in the crypto-world thanks to all those that want to scam the little guy out of their investments. ICOs open and fold in an instant after conning people for investment. Traders take advantage of systems. With the IEO, there is now a change to help eliminate those scams and any one-sided trades that take advantage of people. The best IEOs will provide access to the most reliable, proven companies and secure trades.

A fairer system for newcomers:
There is also the idea that a new IEO may provide a wider variety of options for new traders. Issuers will be able to trade with more freedom and transparency with more potential users. There is also easy access on the side of the new user. This means newcomers can test the waters with greater ease and see what is out there. This new power to the little guy also means that the whales might not get quite so bloated any more.

There have been success stories already with these IEOs.
Binance Launchpad has proved that it is possible to be successful with IEOs. Companies can place their product on the platform, enjoy all the perks, and become successful at the same time. One of the most famous success stories in this switch to the Initial Exchange Offering is GIFTO. This was the very first project on the Launchpad. The idea here is that the platform's 20 million users can send each other virtual gifts. There is nothing much that is too revolutionary about the company, but they will go down in cryptocurrency history

as pioneers in the IEO world. Their success is sure to encourage many other developers to make that leap into this new approach.

Part of the reason for Binance's apparent role in this future success is that they understand all of those benefits mentioned above. They want to improve security for users by implementing a strong application and auditing process. Their structure also means that there is that fairer, more transparent exchange between users. Finally, their reputation in the market means that they keep that sense of integrity and reliability.

Another interesting development in IEOs is the idea that Paraguay wants to get in on the act. There have been rumors that the South American nation is keen to be the leading crypto-market on the continent. The plan is that the government will work with the Blockchain Technology Foundation to create the largest cryptocurrency mining center in the world. They aim to make a start with pre-sale and an IEO.

What is the future for the IEO?
The Initial Exchange Offering is still a pretty new phenomenon. However, there is no doubt that this will continue to grow with time. There will be some miners and whales that worry about this sense of "fairness" and that two-way system. Others may worry that such a strict approach takes users away from the original ideals of cryptocurrency. On the other hand, this new approach could bring in a whole new group of users. It might help to make cryptocurrencies and exchanges more appealing to the wider market. With time, the IEO may change the face of crypto-banking for the better—both at home and further afield in South America.

 The IEO is just one new tool.

There are also those that see the potential in the hybridization of a crypto and stock index. Again, this works on that idea of merging the old, familiar approaches with those that are new and a little more uncertain. A hybrid index would offer access to both typical stock and crypto-markets, placing everything in one easy to access location. This new approach could be an important part of the future of the industry with the right platforms and controls.

So, is there really a future for this hybrid crypto/stock exchange?

As a portfolio manager, when do you start advising to your clients that they have some cryptocurrency exposure? When will there be an index fund, a mutual fund of cryptocurrencies? It will happen.

—MELANIE SWAN

Chapter 18

Crypto & Stock Index For Investors

As we saw above, the best developments in crypto come when we consider a future with solid foundations. That is why it is so important to look at the potential in developing hybrid crypto-stock indexes.

Cryptocurrency indexes are a great tool for investors that want a little helping hand with their options. The idea is that all the best opportunities are presented to the user in a straightforward manner. Users can see the most relevant data on the different currencies and make a more informed choice.

There are a few exchanges that have seen the potential of these indexes and now offer a helpful guide to their investors. Bitmain is surely one of the more influential. They offer real-time spot prices and a daily reference price on the largest cryptocurrencies around. Coinbase was right alongside them but has since seen a bit of an overhaul in its structure. This is fine for now, but there are questions about the potential of a new hybridized approach that will merge a crypto and stock index into one exchange. This may sound ambitious right now, but it isn't that far-fetched.

Why are hybrid exchanges such a welcome step for cryptocurrency investors?

One of the main benefits for users is this idea that they can see all the best data in one place and make comparisons between their options. Or, perhaps more accurately, they can sit back, let these indexes run the numbers and math for them and make choices based on this real-time data. This is a strategy for those that want the quick solution without the effort. This is for those that want every possible tool and index of helpful data at their fingertips. Some may say that this will benefit the whales—providing them with a simple all-you-can-eat buffet. But the right system could help those that are new to the game if they have experience with other trades.

The idea here is that we would see vast indexes of investment opportunities that branch out beyond the crypto-banking world. We would see up-to-date data and rankings on the best cryptocurrencies, but also similar data on other fiat investment and stocks. This is a great idea for all those that want to diversify their portfolio and bring a sense of cohesion to their online dealings. There are people that are already experienced in stock investments and other ventures that turn to cryptocurrency as another addition to their portfolio. At the same time, there could be those that start to get successful with cryptocurrencies that may decide to expand into other territories. An effective crypto-stock index hybrid would provide all that data in one place. It would be the clear, efficient, transparent tool for all these investors.

There is definitely room for expansion here.

With the right acceptance, regulation and a clear system in place, there is no reason why we shouldn't see these hybridized crypto-stock exchanges appearing right across Europe and the US. It may take a little longer in the US, due to all the current issues with regulation and attitudes about keeping crypto and fiat separate. Still, all the major exchanges and players in cryptocurrencies still favor the US dollar. Of course, we can't rule out the East Asian market now that so many companies are keen to tap into this region.

The safest bet here appears to be Central Europe—an area that has already excelled in regard to its acceptance of crypto as a legitimate currency and through its developers. Switzerland's leading stock exchange has begun listing a multi-crypto exchange-traded product. It is listed under HODL and tracks Bitcoin, Ethereum, Ripple, Bitcoin Cash, and Litecoin. The idea is that this ETP will be regulated in precisely the same way as any normal listing. This is big news as SIX Swiss Exchange is the 4th largest in Europe right now. Success with this model could mean more crypto exchanges branching out in their own manner, with broader indexes of different currencies and options. It may prove that it is possible to merge the industries and regulate them equally.

How realistic are these hopes for a truly hybridized crypto-stock exchange?

It may be a while before these functional, user-friendly exchanges become the norm. We need a system that truly provides a clear, unbiased stock and crypto index. This Swiss exchange is a great starting point and should help to influence others.

There is no doubt that cryptocurrencies are becoming more mainstream. New investors want a piece of the action—they want to beat the whales at their own game. This new hybrid index might level the field, but there is another way.

 Of course, there is an alternative to beating the whales at their own game.

You could instead find a way of partnering up with the whales to gain from their trades and expertise. That is precisely what is on offer with the Spiking platform. The aim here isn't to feed into that "us vs. them" mentality with the whales. Instead, there is the chance to use strong whale tracking software to form relationships with them and mirror their trades. There is even an educational program where followers can learn more from these experienced users.

Let's take a closer look at using Spiking to understand those whales.

The massive growth in Ether holdings by active whales could, and most likely is, the result of traders exiting the trading of tokens, most of which have been paired with ETH, which has plummeted by all accounts versus the start of the year.

—DIAR, 26 NOVEMBER 2018

Chapter 19

Using Spiking To Understand Those Whales

Across this series of articles on the future of cryptocurrency, we have spoken a little about the impact of whales. Whales are the giants of the seas, the wise leaders in the ecosystem that can make the biggest impact on its direction. Whales are, therefore, often seen as a problem in the industry. How can new investors ever hope to succeed in cryptocurrency trading when these whales have so much control? This has led to the notion that we should fight against them—make things a little harder for them so that there is a fairer system with bigger gains for all. This sounds great. We all want a better slice of pie when it comes to these new investments. However, this idea of fighting against the whales may be counterproductive.

So what is the solution here?

The solution may be to work with them, rather than against them. There is great potential in working with them, learning from those, and using their presence as a positive force. That is exactly what investors can achieve when they work with this Spiking platform. This is very much the "make love not war" approach to crypto-trading. Why fight these whales when they can be allies? It sounds good in theory, but it requires a little work. That is where this platform comes in.

What can the Spiking platform provide to new users that others can't?

This new platform has been heralded as a leading startup in Singapore and one of the companies to watch. Part of the reason for this is the fact that it does things a little differently. The follower-whale relationships are just the start. Users can also enjoy:

a) new tokens that will be developed as part of a long-term plan.
b) greater trust thanks to the data generated.
c) the chance to enjoy vast profits with the right relationship.
d) educational opportunities for personal development.

The new SPIKE tokens:
The long-term goal of Spiking is to ensure that these SPIKE tokens become a leading cryptocurrency in a strong, decentralized network. There is also the aim to improve technologies and other vital factors in the ecosystem to turn these into a vital resource. This is different from some of those other platforms that don't have much of an endgame in mind.

Improved trust:
Newcomers need to earn the trust of the whale and create a new follower-whale relationship. New users aren't expected to woo a whale in a conventional method. This is all about the best algorithms

and technology. The platform will use credible data to better understand the whale. You can get to know their habits and patterns with a high level of accuracy.

Enhanced profits:
This trust then means the opportunity to mirror the whale's actions via the Spiking Platform. The state-of-the-art system provides an automated transaction system. Followers can form a relationship with a whale based on their previous experience and relevant data. They then mirror the trades to take advantage of that expertise. Once the trade pays off, the whales receive a percentage of the profits as a form of commission. Still, this means a greater chance of success for any experienced users.

Further education:
Granted, we can't learn all that much when we let automated systems simply mirror transactions. That is why the Spiking Certified Smart Trader (C.ST) Program is so important. The information comes from the whales, and new followers can enroll as students. This adds another side to the program that other platforms can't provide. This isn't just about the here and now of the trade. Instead, there is the opportunity to learn and use knowledge to further oneself and improve on trades in the future.

The Public Token Sale for Spiking commenced on December 12th for a duration of 72 hours. The minimum purchase is 0.3 ETH, and the Maximum is 500 ETH. By December 24th, Spiking has sold out public token sale and successfully concluded the Initial Token Offering. New followers that are keen to participate should go over the important guidelines in the chapter on preparing for trading when SPIKE tokens are listed on cryptocurrency exchanges. This is a great opportunity for those that are new to the game. The platform brings together the very best elements of crypto-banking and trading to create something with a real future. Those that invest their time and money here could find that not only are they helping to fund part of the future of the industry, but they are also able to help shape it.

 As you can see, the main goal of this Spiking platform is to provide everything that users need from a modern ICO.

The system is designed to ensure that all those fears of transparency, security, and endgames are put to rest. The secure features, transparent relationships, and clear long-term aims are refreshing in this climate. This Singapore-based company also emphasizes the idea about the Asian market being one to watch in the future. There may be some question marks over the future of cryptocurrency, but this approach shows that there are positive advancements on the horizon.

That is why we need to look at how Spiking can bring the best of crypto-banking to new users.

Like many other companies, Facebook is exploring ways to leverage the power of blockchain technology. This new small team is exploring many different applications. We don't have anything further to share.

—FACEBOOK

Chapter 20

How Spiking Can Bring The Best Of Crypto-Banking To New Users

The Spiking model outlined in the previous chapter is designed to create a beneficial cycle for both the follower and the whale. New followers buy SPIKE tokens in order to follow their whale partner. This gives the whale social influence and a share of the profit on a follower's transactions. Followers are successful by mirroring the whale, earn their investment and continue the cycle. The inner workings of this wheel contain many factors that are greatly needed in the cryptocurrency world. We saw the negative side of modern crypto-banking in previous chapters. Here we have a method that encourages positive change.

Across this guide to the future of cryptocurrency, we have discussed the current problems within the industry. There are many factors that hold companies back and inhibit the expansion of the crypto-ecosystem on a more global level.

These include:
a) the long-term plans of the company.
b) a lack of transparency in the system.
c) issues over the security of fund and users.

Spiking's platform helps to alleviate these concerns.

The beauty of this platform lies in the way that not only does it provide new opportunities for users, but it also helps to reduce these fears. This is a platform where there is no uncertainty over the long-term plan or the scalability of the scheme. There is no concern about relationships and data because of the levels of transparency. Also, there are fewer security fears because of the dedication to a secure, personal system.

Spiking's long-term plans:
As we mentioned before, there are too many companies that are in this for short-term gains and personal profit. Spiking is different because of the emphasis on growth and development. This is a cycle that can only strengthen as whales and followers work together and attract new traders. The addition of the Certified Smart Trader Program means an educational edge that helps users with long-term plans and personal development.

There also has to be a clear endgame, which is why Spiking has published an outline of its plans. Q3 of 2018 was all about the release of the v4.0 of the Spiking Stock Market Exchange app. Q4 2018 is the public sale, the off-chain SPIKE protocol for App Store and Google Play, the mirror trading, and the collection of data on Airflow. Q1 2019 brings the decentralized SPIKE Protocol on multiple cryptocurrency exchanges, the on-chain protocol through Ethereum Blockchain, and the decentralized protocol in external environments. Q2 2019 sees the 1.0 Version of the Commercial product.

Spiking's transparency:
We all need to have trust in the system, whether that means trust in the wider concepts of crypto-banking or trust in the platforms and ICOs we turn towards. Trust comes from transparency. Spiking's follower-whale relationships are based on transparency and the faith that all the important information is out in the open. Spiking is also transparent about their reward system. Followers get 71% of their investments, give a 21% commission to their whale partner and a following 8% to Spiking as a fee. Also, there is transparency over precisely where the contributions from the public sale will go. The plan is that 65% goes to token sales distribution, 20% to the company reserves, 10% into the SPIKE Reconciliation Trading Protocol and 5% to all the advisors, investors, and contributors.

Spiking's security:
Finally, the platform runs with the understanding that secure funds are essential for long-term investments and this ongoing trust. Personal Spiking trading accounts offer this sense of security and the promise of a reliable partnership. Furthermore, there is strong data verification on the whales in these relationships. This is obtained in an effective, decentralized network. Also, the platform has KYC compliance. As we mentioned in the chapter on planning for public sales, this can really help with credibility.

There is a lot about the Spiking platform that makes it seem like a pretty revolutionary approach. The ideas of follower-whale relationship and the educational aspect give this greater depth than other systems. This is something that new followers can invest in, in more ways than one. Yet, many of the approaches are pretty obvious when it comes to improving the future of the cryptocurrency industry. The notions here simply help to remove some of the problems of the past and create that secure, appealing space that users want.

Conclusion

The Future of Cryptocurrency Isn't As Dark As It May Seem

When we talk about the future of cryptocurrency and the potential of the industry, there are two viewpoints that we need to consider. We can't overlook all those that still fear this approach. This is still a scary market for many newcomers. The volatile nature isn't going to disappear overnight. Still, there are many others that have strong ideas and platforms that can steer the crypto-world in the right direction. Many see the potential for growth and stability with the help of the right government regulations and funders.

It is understandable that many people will be concerned about various aspects of cryptocurrency and crypto-banking. There are some valid criticisms about companies that have come and gone. Many new investors have fallen foul to the scams of dodgy ICOs. Then there are those that read into the lack of regulation and government support and all those spikes and crashes in the market. The best currencies have crashed and will continue to rise and fall, much like a "regular" fiat currency. Even the biggest giants aren't immune to this. Still, there is hope that changes in regulations and attitudes could help users see a new side to cryptocurrencies. A more regulated, transparent approach with better relationship could reduce some of that volatility in the long term.

New attitudes mean that the world is opening its eyes a little more.

Eastern markets like Singapore could be the way forward. For a long time, the eyes of the crypto-banking world fell upon the US and Europe. Some of the best ICO creators were based in the UK and

Central Europe. The US was a focus due to the fixation on the dollar as a fiat trading currency. Ongoing issues with regulators and US law meant that the US stayed in the spotlight. But then, investors and developers began to spread their wings. Binance's ventures in Uganda and Singapore were proof that the crypto-world was larger than it seemed. Paraguay began talks about mining. China began loosening its laws. This acceptance and expansion can only continue as companies test the waters and prove their worth.

There are companies and ICOs out there looking to change the game.

There is a lot of talk about the importance of the endgame in the future of the industry. There is no longer room for the short-term approach where companies meet their crowd-funding goals, set up a token and have no means of developing or marketing the brand. Developers need to have the skills to see the bigger picture. They need to understand where the business is heading—with branding, tech development, and the possibility of switching to IPOs in the future. They also need to have the transparency and communication to ensure that investors are aware of these aims. Platforms like Spiking show that this is possible. Their clear game plan and the clear relationships between whales and followers put it on track to be a game changer.

Perhaps closer relationships and whale tracking is the better approach to secure the future of the cryptocurrency industry. The issues that users are most afraid of are the lack of security, the uncertainty over their investment and the inability to compete in this competitive world. Once developers and exchange understand this, and have the regulatory backing to proceed, they can use these strong, user-friendly platforms to transform the industry. Nothing is ever set in stone in the financial world. There is always going to be some form of a high-risk/high-reward venture in these trades and investments. Still, a little more stability, security, and knowledge will go a long way.

There is a strong future here with the right approach.

With the right developers and funders behind the wheel, the future of cryptocurrency could be brighter than we think. That is why new investors are encouraged to join in at the ground level. Find the most appealing currency, secure yourself with the right wallet, and invest in the best opportunities. Before long, you could be riding the same waves as the biggest whales—tracking them and learning from them as you go. If that isn't a sign of positive progression in the industry, then what is?

With faith, hope, and love,
CLEMEN CHIANG

Acknowledgements

It was more than 15 years ago when I first started my entrepreneurial journey. Looking back, I am so grateful to my family who supported my decision to pursue this path. Top on the list begins with my true love, my awesome wife, Nicole Yee—my soul mate. She's my anchor and I would be so lost without her. I feel that God put her in my life for a reason—to make me laugh with joy and to guide me spiritually. As it was stated in Proverbs 5:18, "Let your wife be a fountain of blessing for you." I am truly blessed with the love of this kind heart. To each of my three boys, Yee, Le, Loong, you have given me so much happiness and hope. I pray that each of you will grow up to pursue life passionately. To my Papa and Mama, thank you for raising me up and supporting me when I am down. Papa—you're my number one fan for showing up in all my events. To Nicole's Pa and Ma, thank you for caring for me and our boys. Your love, faith and prayers matter. To my sister Lissa and my brother-in-law Bryan (whom I watched you grow up), thank you for believing in me. And to my extended family, I love you all.

To my team at Spiking, it's such a privilege to have the best talents in Singapore and Saint Petersburg working together to build fintech and blockchain products that empower investors worldwide. To Reuben (whom I treat as my brother)—my confidant who look out for me all these years. To my outstanding product team led by Alexey—Paul, Pasha, Valeria, Anastasia, Maxim, and Renat, thank you for solving all the backlogs with patience and commits you push to Github with love! To Michael, Adrien, Andrey, Widelia—you are amazing, loyal, and steadfast. To our remarkable advisors—Charles, Minh, James, Ying, Peter, Caleb, Eric, Eugene, Kenneth, Jack, Andy, Ouyang, Hitters, Zachary, Rune, Charlie—thank you to each of you for all that you do in our quest to "get the power of 1,000 whales in your wallet." To William, The Genius, thank you for your generosity in imparting your wisdom. To Jeremy, my sparring budding and prayer warrior, thank you for your friendship.

To my distinguished supporters, it's my highest honor to receive your support in the form of investment. More than monetary value itself, you have given us encouragement, inspiration, leadership—uplifted us to a higher calling. James, Kazumasa, Fook Moy, Stanley, Dragon, Sammi, Lee, Julian, Ronnie, Chu Poh, MC, Soon Huat, Simon, Lisa, Andrew, Cheng Guan, Douglas, Carl, Bryan, Boon Hwee, Chow Boon, Kiat Wang, and Houyi. Thank you from the bottom of my heart and we will not let you down.

To our extraordinary partners who are Samaritans at different seasons, deepest thanks for making a huge difference. Our community managers led by Jun Yi—Axel, Clarence, James, Jin, and Sean. You guys rock! Our public relations team—Corinne and Ronnie—thank you for your prayers, guidance, and love.

Finally, and most importantly, I thank all our Spiking fans and users, without whom there is no reason for building the products and writing this book. On this day, I give thanks to the Lord, and I continue to pray for a miracle to take place in your life. So that you will experience Spiking—your freedom.

About The Author

This book comes to you from Clemen Chiang, Ph.D., he has been an avid investor in the stock market since the 2000s. His 15+ years of experience in trading and the finer details of the financial market prepared him well for the development of the cryptocurrency industry. In addition to this, Dr. Chiang has many educational qualifications, including his Bachelor of Engineering from Nanyang Technological University, an MBA from the University of Louisville, and a Ph.D. from the University of Canberra.

The growth of this emerging market is one that he follows with great interest, and his insights have proved influential for future investments and partnerships. He can often be found at major conferences and expos, giving inspirational talks to those that want to share in his wisdom. He is rated as a top investment coach by

Nielsen//NetRatings and is an active member of ICObench community as a leading ICObench expert.

His knowledge on the inner workings of the cryptocurrency industry has influenced his work as a writer. He has been able to take all he has learned and the insights from across the industry to create his series on The Future Of Cryptocurrency. His work is available on Medium, the Spiking.io site, and other leading online publications.

Dr. Chiang also works as an advisor to COSS, IGT-CRYPTO, and 1SG. This new book is an opportunity for Dr. Chiang to bring together his experience and insights into an easy-to-digest form. It is another part of his aim to help make cryptocurrencies more appealing and understandable for a wider audience.

His knowledge and expertise have also led to the creation of Spiking. Dr. Chiang is the CEO and Co-founder of this new platform, along with Nicole Yee. The Spiking platform is the result of their hard work, experience, and relationships with other traders and developers. They have also gained support for the project from the National Research Foundation of Singapore Prime Minister's Office. The Spiking Platform is set to revolutionize the way that traders and whales interact and enjoy safer, more profitable trades.

Dr. Chiang's role in this platform has cemented his position as one of the leading developers and authorities in the Singapore cryptocurrency industry. Back in 2016, Dr. Chiang and his team received the Gold award for Best Innovative Start-up at the SiTF Awards 2016 by the Singapore Infocomm Technology Federation. Since then, his reputation and related accolades have grown. Spiking has received a great reaction from the press. *Singapore Business Review* called the platform one of Singapore's 20 hottest startups to watch in 2017.

All of this experience in the industry—both with fiat trading and cryptocurrency trading—means that Clemen Chiang is well-versed in the issues that shape the future of cryptocurrency. He has witnessed the rise and fall of major currencies, the stumbling blocks and regulations of different regions and many companies that came and went along the way. He understands the role of Singapore, and Asian markets more generally in the future of the industry. In addition to this, he has his role in Spiking as a strong, firsthand experience of the current status of the industry. This long tenure and diverse skill set show that he is more than qualified to write this book and offer insight into the future of the cryptocurrency market.

References

Chapter 1
- https://themerkle.com/top-10-cryptocurrency-icos-throughout-2017-to-date/
- https://www.forbes.com/sites/ajagrawal/2017/09/20/6-tips-on-marketing-an-ico/#6fa80922c37f
- https://landerapp.com/blog/5-keys-to-do-white-paper-marketing-the-right-way/
- https://www.forbes.com/sites/ajagrawal/2017/11/06/3-keys-to-building-a-marketing-plan-for-an-ico/#9a7a0844e299
- https://hackernoon.com/what-to-look-for-in-an-ico-white-paper-successful-token-54eba3787139

Chapter 2
- http://belfrics.com/blog/best-5-bitcoin-exchanges-worldwide
- https://www.coinbase.com
- https://www.finder.com/sg/cryptocurrency/exchanges
- https://www.buybitcoinworldwide.com/exchanges/coinbase/
- https://www.forexbrokerz.com/brokers/belfrics-review
- https://www.buybitcoinworldwide.com/exchanges/coinmama/
- http://blockgeeks.com/guides/what-is-blockchain-technology/

Chapter 3
- https://finance.yahoo.com/news/amid-2018-crypto-crash-3-kinds-believers-come-focus-202424977.html
- https://coingape.com/bitcoin-market-making-detailed-study-reveals
- https://www.cnbc.com/2018/09/03/china-clamps-down-on-cryptocurrency-speculation.html
- https://www.bizjournals.com/bizjournals/how-to/growth-strategies/2017/03/how-old-money-and-new-money-habits-differ.html

Chapter 4
- https://www.coss.io

Chapter 5
- https://www.cnbc.com/2018/03/27/a-complete-guide-to-cyprocurrency-regulations-around-the-world.html
- https://freestartupkits.com/articles/technology/cryptocurrency-news-and-tips/best-crypto-friendly-banks/
- https://www.ft.com/content/c2098ef6-ff84-11e7-9650-9c0ad2d7c5b5
- https://www.tearsheet.co/future-of-investing/why-banking-startups-are-rolling-out-crypto-products
- https://www.bloomberg.com/news/articles/2017-12-08/the-bitcoin-whales-1-000-people-who-own-40-percent-of-the-market

Chapter 6
- https://bravenewcoin.com/insights/what-are-security-tokens-and-how-will-they-transform-icos
- https://www.forbes.com/sites/rachelwolfson/2018/09/16/institutional-investors-bet-on-crypto-market-with-tokenized-securities/#4427933b7a48
- https://coinreport.net/security-token-offerings-part3/

Chapter 7
- https://www.theguardian.com/technology/2018/sep/11/stable-coins-bitcoin-cryptocurrencies-tether
- https://cointelegraph.com/news/two-us-audited-stablecoins-debut-experts-see-massive-impact-on-crypto-market
- https://www.forbes.com/sites/shermanlee/2018/03/12/explaining-stable-coins-the-holy-grail-of-crytpocurrency/#101e3b244fc6

Chapter 8
- https://www.forbes.com/sites/billybambrough/2018/09/06/bitcoin-could-be-boosted-by-a-new-potential-etf/#2c74a49754a5

- https://cointelegraph.com/news/cnbcs-ran-neuner-says-bitcoin-is-about-to-explode-points-to-pending-etf-decision
- https://bitcoinist.com/the-sec-sets-deadline-to-file-comments-for-or-against-bitcoin-etf-applications/
- https://www.ccn.com/why-did-the-sec-reject-all-derivative-backed-bitcoin-etfs/
- https://www.fool.com/investing/2018/09/17/bitcoin-etfs-have-a-supporter-at-the-sec.aspx https://www.ccn.com/sec-halts-u-s-trading-of-swedish-bitcoin-etf-bitcoin-markets-not-impacted/

Chapter 9
- https://www.newsbtc.com/2018/10/11/ethereum-price-analysis-eth-usd-down-and-out-below-key-support/
- https://bitcoinexchangeguide.com/ripple-vs-ethereum-cryptocurrency-race-for-top-2-spot-xrp-vs-eth-2018-analysis/
- https://medium.com/futuresin/why-ethereum-is-the-future-of-blockchain-950a5c56f524
- https://techcrunch.com/2017/06/08/how-ethereum-became-the-platform-of-choice-for-icod-digital-assets/
- https://coingape.com/ethereum-litecoin-could-join-the-us-futures-market/

Chapter 10
- https://www.coininsider.com/what-is-a-token-swap/
- https://www.ccn.com/tether-has-yanked-610-million-out-of-circulation-this-month/
- https://blockwolf.com/token-swaps-and-atomic-swaps-explained/
- https://bitcoinexchangeguide.com/why-you-should-expect-ethereum-to-eventually-hit-zero-the-ultimate-eth-bear-case/

Chapter 11
- https://www.coindesk.com/over-half-of-icos-fail-within-4-months-suggests-us-study/
- https://hackernoon.com/4-primary-reasons-why-icos-fail-43274fd34e2e

- https://www.coindesk.com/death-ico-4-2018-predictions/
- https://techcrunch.com/2018/05/03/telegrams-billion-dollar-ico-has-become-a-mess/
- https://www.finder.com/uk/initial-coin-offerings
- http://todaysgazette.com/bitmain-files-18-billion-ipo/

Chapter 12

- https://globalcoinreport.com/ripple-innovative-bitcoin-degraded-ccid-new-crypto-rankings/ https://www.icoexaminer.com/ico-news/chinese-court-rules-bitcoin-is-lawful/
- https://news.bitcoin.com/ico-activity-down/
- https://www.forbes.com/sites/stevenehrlich/2018/09/17/making-sense-of-chinas-grand-blockchain-strategy/#76cbb7af3678
- https://smartereum.com/7630/how-alibaba-is-championing-the-application-of-blockchain-technology-in-china-and-beyond-sun-nov-04/

Chapter 13

- https://www.bloomberg.com/news/articles/2018-10- 23/temaseks-vertex-invests-in-binance-to-expand-in-singapore
- http://digestafrica.com/government- singaporeinvesting-binance/#.W-BBieKYTIU
- https://www.newsbtc.com/2018/11/01/singapore-launches-token-day-to-bring-crypto-to-the-masses/
- https://www.coindesk.com/uganda-africa-binance-crypto-unbanked-traders/ h
- ttps://usethebitcoin.com/list-of-most-crypto-friendly-cities-in-the-world/

Chapter 14

- https://bitcoinexchangeguide.com/initial-coin-offerings-ico-provide-significant-advantages-over-initial-public-offerings-ipo/
- https://bitcoinist.com/cryptocurrency-ipo-capped-900-million/
- https://bitcoinist.com/bitfury-bitcoin-mining-ipo/
- https://bitnewstoday.com/news/exchange/illusions-perdues-in-economics-the-majority-is-always-wrong/

Chapter 15

- https://www.coindesk.com/crypto-exchange-btcc-is-closing-its-mining-pool-business-indefinitely
- https://www.smartcompany.com.au/technology/how-to-prevent-cryptomining-attacks/
- https://www.coindesk.com/bitmain-faces-5-million-lawsuit-over-alleged-unauthorized-crypto-mining
- https://www.ccn.com/coinmarketcap-removes-volume-requirements-for-cryptocurrency-exchange-listing/
- https://www.reddit.com/r/CryptoCurrency/comments/7pdxvc/coinmarketcap_mining_xmr_on_everyones_computer/

Chapter 16

- https://medium.com/menlo-one/how-to-participate-in-an-ico-step-by-step-guide-to-a-token-sale-43fa537254da
- https://medium.com/@woodforklaw/what-is-kyc-b8fc42ea4df
- https://blockchainhub.net/how-to-participate-in-an-ico-token-sale/
- https://www.coinstaker.com/ico-presale-pre-ico/

Chapter 17

- https://www.livebitcoinnews.com/binance-launchpad-announces-gifto-inaugural-ico-project/
- https://medium.com/consentium/the-initial-community-offering-9f626395622e
- https://medium.com/traceto-io/what-is-an-initial-exchange-offering-ieo-245a7cf72f28
- https://usethebitcoin.com/paraguay-home-largest-crypto-mining-farm/

Chapter 18

- https://www.coindesk.com/mining-giant-bitmain-launches-crypto-index-for-investors
- https://cointelegraph.com/news/major-swiss-stock-exchange-six-lists-the-worlds-first-crypto-etp-amidst-market-collapse

- https://www.fxstreet.com/cryptocurrencies/news/cryptocurrency-index-funds-crypto-for-lazy-investors-201811270935

Chapter 19
- https://spiking.io/
- https://blog.spiking.com

Chapter 20
- https://spiking.io/
- https://blog.spiking.com

Permissions

Book Cover Illustration: By permission of Denis Luther Antoine Yahnick / Cointelegraph

Book Cover Design: By Paul Alexandrov / Spiking

Editorial Credit: Richie Chan / Shutterstock.com

This book is designed to provide information that the author believes to be accurate on the subject matter it covers, but it is sold with the understanding that neither the author nor the publisher is offering individualized advice tailored to any specific portfolio or to any individual's particular needs, or rendering investment advice or other professional services such as legal or accounting advice. A competent professional services should be sought if one needs expert assistance in areas that include investment, legal, and accounting advice.

This publication references performance data collected over many time periods. Past results do not guarantee future performance. Additionally, performance data, in addition to laws and regulations, change over time, which could change the status of the information in this book. This book solely provides historical data to discuss and illustrate the underlying principles. Additionally, this book is not intended to serve as the basis for any financial decision; as a recommendation of a specific investment advisor; or as an offer to sell or purchase any security or cryptocurrency. Only a prospectus may be used to offer to sell or purchase securities, and a prospectus must be read and considered carefully before investing or spending money.

No warranty is made with respect to the accuracy or completeness of the information contained herein, and both the author and the publisher specifically disclaim any responsibility for any liability, loss, or risk, personal or otherwise, which is incurred as a consequence, directly or indirectly, of the use and application of any of the contents of this book.

In the text that follows, many people's names and identifying characteristics have been changed.

Spiking

Spiking Limited
Cassia Court, Camana Bay,
Suite 716
10 Market Street, Grand Cayman
KY1-9006, Cayman Islands
www.Spiking.com

Copyright © 2018 by Clemen Chiang

All rights reserved, including the right to reproduce this book or portions thereof in any form whatsoever. For information address Spiking Limited Paperbacks Subsidiary Rights Department, Cassia Court, Camana Bay, Suite 716, 10 Market Street, Grand Cayman KY1-9006, Cayman Islands.

Spiking can bring the author to your live event.

For more information or to book an event, contact Spiking Limited at 65-61000259 or visit our website at www.Spiking.com

Interior design by Paul Alexandrov / Spiking

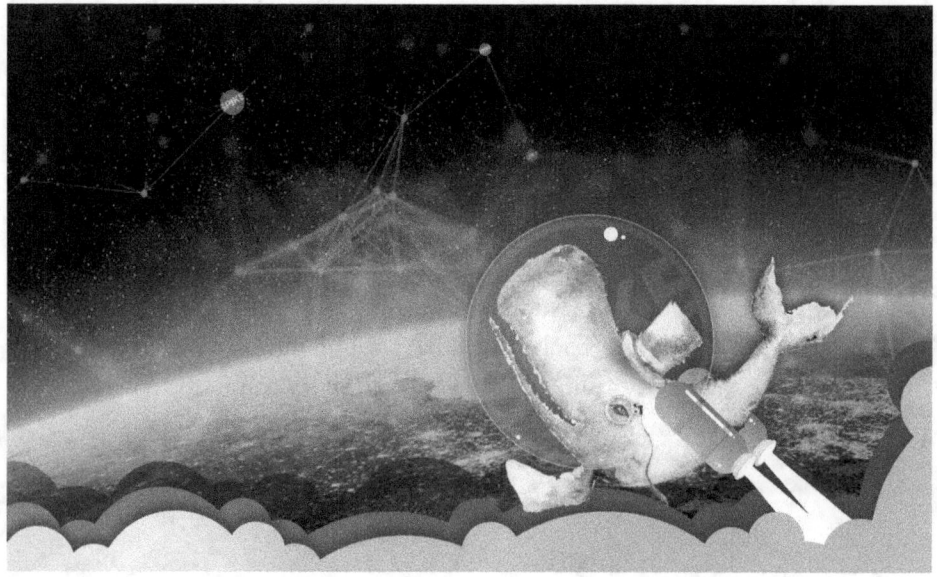

www.ingramcontent.com/pod-product-compliance
Lightning Source LLC
Chambersburg PA
CBHW051315220526
45468CB00004B/1350